D0823369

Praying for Justice

A Lectionary of Christian Concern

R. Anderson Campbell and Steve Sherwood

with Paula J. Hampton

BARCLAY PRESS
Newberg, OR 97132

Praying For Justice:
A Lectionary of Christian Concern

© 2017 by R. Anderson Campbell and Steve Sherwood

Barclay Press, Inc.
Newberg, Oregon
www.barclaypress.com

Scripture quotations taken from the New American Standard Bible® (NASB),
Copyright © 1960, 1962, 1963, 1968, 1971, 1972, 1973, 1975, 1977, 1995 by The
Lockman Foundation. Used by permission. www.Lockman.org

Scripture quotations marked (NIV) are taken from the Holy Bible, New
International Version®, NIV®. Copyright © 1973, 1978, 1984, 2011 by Biblica,
Inc.™ Used by permission of Zondervan. All rights reserved worldwide. www.
zondervan.com The "NIV" and "New International Version" are trademarks
registered in the United States Patent and Trademark Office by Biblica, Inc.™
All rights reserved.

Scripture quotations marked (NRSV) are taken from the New Revised Standard
Version Bible, copyright © 1989 National Council of the Churches of Christ in
the United States of America. Used by permission.

ISBN 978-1-59498-038-1

COVER ART BY ELISABETH LICITRA
COVER DESIGN BY NICOLE FAWVER

Acknowledgments

This book was conceived in the days following the end of the 2016 presidential election cycle. Weary from the vicious rhetoric and concerned about how to move forward in a positive, constructive way, we took up this project. In order to have this book in your hands before the incoming president took office, we needed to gather more than fourteen hundred Scripture verses, more than two hundred quotations from theologians and ministry practitioners, put them in some semblance of order, and then check, recheck, and recheck again all the work we'd done. We gave ourselves three weeks.

It would have been impossible for just the two of us to do this on our own, so we sent out a call for assistance. We were astounded at the response. Dozens of people offered to help in their spare time.

Thank you, first and foremost, to our administrative assistant, Paula Hampton. Her experience as a copy editor and her commitment to accuracy and expediency was indispensable. She freely shared her logistical expertise as we struggled in the first few days with how to even approach a project as large as this on such a short timeline, and she contributed a number of excellent quotations as well. In addition, she supervised and directed a number of enterprising, dedicated work-study students as they combed through our work, catching and correcting numerous mistakes: Taylor Staman, Zack Tewksbury, Mercie Hodges, Miranda Edwords, and Courtney Bither, thank you.

We would like to thank David Sherwood, who turned his experienced editorial eye to the introduction and acknowledgments and our colleague Paul Anderson and university president Robin Baker who offered insightful feedback on the introduction.

A lot of the help we received came from people to whom we are connected through social media, who liked the idea of this project and wanted to support it. Jessy Hampton, Rochelle Deans, Arturo Lucatero, Steve Lewis, Gus Cole-Kroll, Chris Morris, Carmen Imes, and Rachelle Staley—there is no way we could have done this without your help.

We owe a big debt of gratitude to Eric Muhr and the whole Barclay Press team. Most publishing houses would not have been able to turn this book around in time to get it in the hands of the public by Inauguration Day 2017. Eric and his team worked their magic and made our dream a physical reality.

Even with all of these helping hands, the tight weeks of production meant that the two of us often worked during every spare moment, for days on end. In light of that, we owe a profound debt of thanks to our spouses, Elizabeth Meeker Sherwood and April Campbell, as well as our children. Not only were they patient and indulgent during our absence from family life during these days, but they were enthusiastically supportive of the project.

Finally, we would like to thank you. By picking up this book, you are aligning yourself with God's heart for "the least" in our society. Nothing could make us happier.

Introduction

It's easy to look at the campaign rhetoric during the previous eighteen months and conclude that the next four years are going to be profoundly difficult for the vulnerable in our society. The reality is that, for them, every year is difficult. Most of the Founding Fathers were slaveholders. Franklin Delano Roosevelt interred more than one hundred thousand Japanese American citizens. Liberal and conservative presidents led a country that for decades allowed Jim Crow laws to remain in place and denied women the right to vote. John Fitzgerald "Jack" Kennedy dragged his feet on civil rights reform. Ronald Reagan's policies on mental health led to an explosion in the number of homeless in our country. Bill Clinton ushered in the mass incarceration of young African Americans. Barack Obama has deported more undocumented immigrants than any president before him. If one is convinced, as we are, that God's heart is uniquely for those without power, without recourse to justice, then there has never been a time in our nation's history when the powers that be have been in alignment with this passion of God's.

We believe God is uniquely concerned for the vulnerable: the refugee, the immigrant, the unborn and those born into economic hardship, the former mill worker struggling to find a way forward, and the young black man hoping to get home safely. Their desperation and fear is just as real and just as much God's concern as the fear felt by undocumented citizens and refugees. The recent election cycle has made this misalignment both visible and visceral, but it has always been there. God is on the side of the vulnerable, no matter the source or cause.

The genesis of this book was three days after the 2016 election when one of us (Steve) was glumly riding an exercise bike in the early morning hours, following three nights of poor sleep. Convinced that merely ranting about the election on social media wasn't going to help, he hit upon an idea: "I'm just going to post a verse a day, for four years, with each one being about God's concern for the poor and marginalized." Arriving at work that Friday morning, and talking to his colleague (Anderson) at the university where they both teach, the two quickly decided that something like that would take some organization and that others might like access to those verses, too. An innocent Facebook post—"If we put together a list of Bible passages about God's heart for the marginalized and for justice, along with maybe a few quotes from others, would you be interested in that?"—led, in a couple hours, to a few hundred enthusiastic responses of, "Yes, please!" And with that, this book was born.

You will note that this book begins on a rather odd date: January 20, 2017, Inauguration Day. It ends the day before the next presidential inauguration in 2021. Why tie this book to a specific period of time—a presidential term—instead of any four-year period? We believe there is something powerful in praying for specific people during specific times, and the vitriol of this particular campaign cycle has struck us as especially disconcerting. That is not to say that this book hasn't been needed during previous presidential terms or won't be needed in the future. Perhaps future editions will appear without these specific date headers. It happens that we find ourselves near the beginning of a new president's term with questions about how this president—indeed any president—will lead when it comes to the oppressed, the marginalized and the poor.

The title of this book contains an invitation to pray for justice, but this book contains no overt prayers. Many of the more than fourteen hundred passages contained here are prayers, or portions of prayers recorded in the Bible. To read these texts is to be invited to join them in prayer. The quotations that we have included are unapologetically Christian. With the exception of one or two, all are penned by people of the Christian faith, who have spent their lives thinking about, working for, and telling others about a God who they believe to be radically on the side of the weak, vulnerable, and marginalized. We scoured our shelves for a diverse range of perspectives, actively working to ensure that we included as many kinds of voices as we could. Our hope is that their words will also be a call to pray for the people and causes they write about. The invitation throughout this book is to use each day's verse as a meditation or reflection for that day and each week's quotation as a way of examining the ways in which your life images God's redemptive justice in the world.

Where possible, we chose gender neutral translations of verses. Where that wasn't possible, you will note our use of brackets to indicate minor changes intended to help isolated verses read more inclusively. We have also employed brackets to clarify some verses, when such clarity was lost by removing the verse from its original context. Aside from the intentional placing of some quotations on significant Christian or civic dates, we have randomly assigned the passages and quotations to the days and weeks in which you find them. The result is that, in a given week, you may find verses that reflect attitudes of joy, anger, fear, or hope. To us, that feels a lot like a normal week. If you come upon a passage or quotation that doesn't "speak to your condition" (to use a phrase from the Quaker leader George Fox), just skip over it.

Some of the verses invite more context. It's impossible here to adequately frame each verse. That said, perhaps a few very broad brush strokes might help. Starting with the call of Abraham, continuing through the story of Moses leading the Hebrew people out of slavery in Egypt, and through the kingdom of Israel's tumultuous history, the Old Testament tells a story of the formation of a particular kind of nation, and more significantly, the story of a different kind of God. Repeatedly, God asks the Israelites to be a people different than the nations around them. Over and over again they are called to act with compassion for immigrants, the poor, and the vulnerable because "you were once slaves in Egypt, and

I brought you out from there." This dynamic—because you have known suffering, you must act with kindness and mercy—pervades the Old Testament narrative. Unfortunately, Israel often suffered from kings and outside powers that acted in oppressive or violent ways. In response, God sent prophets to "speak truth to power," advocating to these kings and powers on behalf of the vulnerable whose voices were silenced. A vast number of the passages in this book come from either God's instruction to the Israelites regarding mercy and compassion, or from the prophets' often angry reminder to those in power that when it comes to justice, God means business.

When we picture the vulnerable in our society, we think of people of color, undocumented immigrants, victims of sexual assault or harassment, Syrian refugees, the unborn, and LGTBQI people. Reading the Bible, one quickly discovers that these specific groups are not mentioned, or at least not named with the same names we use today. Instead, one often encounters comments about *widows and orphans, sojourners in your midst, the poor.* In a sense, these are catch-all phrases for people lacking advocacy, power, or options. These were people vulnerable to the machinations of *the wicked* in the Bible. All of that is reflected in our biblical excerpts. It is appropriate to read into and expand these categories to include all of the vulnerable people in our present societal moment.

Righteousness appears often in our collection. In American Christianity, it can be tempting to think of "righteousness" in terms of personal morality, like sexual purity and the avoidance of drugs and alcohol, or in terms of positive behaviors like going to church and reading the Bible. While important, none of these descriptions portray what people in the time during which the Bible was written would have understood as *righteousness.* It becomes clear as you read verse after verse in this collection, biblical *righteousness* has a deeply relational aspect to it. It is a concept built around healthy relationships, between individuals, and within the community.

Peace is another term making dozens of appearances. Both of the authors have strong connections to the peace church movement. Too often, even within peace church circles, the idea of "peace" brings to mind simply a state of non-conflict, which is a woefully inadequate understanding of this rich biblical term. *Shalom,* in a biblical sense, is infinitely more than mere non-conflict. It is wholeness, things-as-they-should-be, a sense of health and well-being pervading every element of society. When Jesus is called the "Prince of Peace," it is a bold declaration that he has come to set the world aright, not merely end human conflict. As you encounter *peace* over and over in the book, try to read in its place this rich, dripping-with-goodness idea of *shalom.*

By focusing on verses and quotations that highlight issues of social justice, are we suggesting that this is all God cares about? What about salvation, doctrine, sexual morality? Let us be clear: the Bible indicates that God does care about all of those things and much more. In choosing not to address them here, we are not suggesting that these are not worthy topics of concern. But let us also be clear that in the Bible there is no cluster of moral issues that God expresses more concern for than how we treat one another economically, socially, and communally. The Bible places issues of social compassion and justice at the moral and ethical center of its teaching, and we think that Christians likewise need to center their moral and ethical actions in these concerns.

Finally, this book is a call to action. As German pastor and theologian Dietrich Bonhoeffer, writing to Christians in Nazi Germany, and Martin Luther King, Jr., writing to Christian pastors from a jail cell in Birmingham, Alabama, both admonished: injustice and oppression can be served by the passivity of otherwise good people who refuse to act or speak up in the face of actions by those who abuse power. There is never a time for Christians to sit and trust that others will take care of people on the margins of our society. The institution where we work, George Fox University, is named for the founder of the Religious Society of Friends. Fox famously refused to remove his hat when he stood before the king, and the Society of Friends has a long tradition of speaking truth to power, as an historic peace-church and early adopter of both prison reform and the abolition movement. And yet, George Fox University is a diverse institution. The particular sentiments expressed in this introduction are not universally shared among our colleagues, and our role as teaching faculty should in no way imply that our university officially endorses this project. Our prayer is that the next four years will be a time during which Christians from all denominational backgrounds and political parties will not content themselves with mere social media activism or personal piety, *but will act*. Act often. Act publicly. Act sacrificially. Act with courage and compassion. Act as if it matters—because it does.

R. Anderson Campbell
Steve Sherwood
Advent, 2016

100 percent of the net proceeds of this book go to Church World Service to aid in their work resettling refugees and advocating for immigrant and refugee rights in the United States.

2017

Week 1: January 20-21, 2017

People are free to choose the political system they want, but not free to do whatever they feel like. They will have to be judged by God's justice in the political or social system they choose. God is the judge of all social systems. Neither the gospel nor the church can be monopolized by any political or social movement.

Oscar A. Romero
The Violence of Love (119)

Friday, January 20 - *Inauguration Day*

Vindicate me, my God, and plead my cause against an unfaithful nation. Rescue me from those who are deceitful and wicked. *Psalm 43:1 (NIV)*

Saturday, January 21

Rise up, Lord, confront them, bring them down; with your sword rescue me from the wicked. *Psalm 17:13 (NIV)*

Week 2: January 22-28, 2017

There can be no love apart from suffering. Love demands that we expose ourselves at our most vulnerable point by keeping the heart open.

Howard Thurman
Mysticism and the Experience of Love (21)

Sunday, January 22

For You save an afflicted people, but haughty eyes You abase. *Psalm 18:27 (NASB)*

Monday, January 23

He knew what they were thinking and said to them, "Every kingdom divided against itself is laid waste, and no city or house divided against itself will stand." *Matthew 12:25 (NRSV)*

Tuesday, January 24

For You have been a defense for the helpless, a defense for the needy in [their] distress, a refuge from the storm, a shade from the heat. *Isaiah 25:4a (NASB)*

Wednesday, January 25

You have wearied the Lord with your words. Yet you say, "How have we wearied [the Lord]?" By saying, "All who do evil are good in the sight of the Lord, and [the Lord] delights in them." Or by asking, "Where is the God of justice?" *Malachi 2:17 (NRSV)*

Thursday, January 26

Oppressing the poor in order to enrich oneself, and giving to the rich, will lead only to loss. *Proverbs 22:16 (NRSV)*

Friday, January 27

Evening, morning and noon I cry out in distress, and [God] hears my voice. *Psalm 55:17 (NIV)*

Saturday, January 28

Each of us must please our neighbor for the good purpose of building up the neighbor. *Romans 15:2 (NRSV)*

Week 3: January 29—February 4, 2017

Love makes it necessary to find the way of truth, understanding, justice and peace. My kind of religion is a very active, highly political, often controversial, and sometimes very dangerous form of engagement in active nonviolence for the transformation of our world.

Jean Zaru
Occupied with Nonviolence:
A Palestinian Woman Speaks (7)

Sunday, January 29

Moreover, Absalom would say, "Oh that one would appoint me judge in the land, then every[one] who has any suit or cause could come to me and I would give [them] justice." *2 Samuel 15:4 (NASB)*

Monday, January 30

If then you have not been faithful with the dishonest wealth, who will entrust to you the true riches? *Luke 16:11 (NRSV)*

Tuesday, January 31

But as for me, I am poor and needy; come quickly to me, O God. You are my help and my deliverer; Lord, do not delay. *Psalm 70:5 (NIV)*

Wednesday, February 1

When the wicked are in authority, transgression increases, but the righteous will look upon their downfall. *Proverbs 29:16 (NRSV)*

Thursday, February 2

The Lord is far from the wicked, but [God] hears the prayer of the righteous. *Proverbs 15:29 (NRSV)*

Friday, February 3

It is better to be of a lowly spirit among the poor than to divide the spoil with the proud. *Proverbs 16:19 (NRSV)*

Saturday, February 4

Therefore, thus says the Lord God, "Behold, My servants will eat, but you will be hungry. Behold, My servants will drink, but you will be thirsty. Behold, My servants will rejoice, but you will be put to shame." *Isaiah 65:13 (NASB)*

Week 4: February 5-11, 2017

Whatever liberation our churches bring to others must come not from our exertion of alternate (specifically oppressive) powers, but from the tabernacling of God in our particular community, guiding us to distinct ways to love our neighbors.

Marva J. Dawn
Powers, Weakness, and
the Tabernacling of God (154)

Sunday, February 5

Who cause a person to be indicted by a word, and ensnare [them] who adjudicate at the gate, and defraud the one in the right with meaningless arguments. *Isaiah 29:21 (NASB)*

Monday, February 6

[Evildoers] eat the bread of wickedness and drink the wine of violence. *Proverbs 4:17 (NRSV)*

Tuesday, February 7

Instruct those who are rich in this present world not to be conceited or to fix their hope on the uncertainty of riches, but on God, who richly supplies us with all things to enjoy. *1 Timothy 6:17 (NASB)*

Wednesday, February 8

The Lord is good, a stronghold in a day of trouble; [the Lord] protects those who take refuge in [God]. *Nahum 1:7 (NRSV)*

Thursday, February 9

Now King Solomon levied forced laborers from all Israel; and the forced laborers numbered 30,000 men. *1 Kings 5:13 (NASB)*

Friday, February 10

Every tree that does not bear good fruit is cut down and thrown into the fire. Thus you will know them by their fruits. *Matthew 7:19-20 (NRSV)*

Saturday, February 11

Why has the way of the wicked prospered? Why are all those who deal in treachery at ease? *Jeremiah 12:1b (NASB)*

Week 5: February 12-18, 2017

So what is the response of the white evangelical community to the changing face of America? So far, it has been one of conspicuous silence on the issue of immigration.

Soong-Chan Rah
The Next Evangelicalism (75)

Sunday, February 12

The Lord gives strength to his people; the Lord blesses [the Lord's] people with peace. *Psalm 29:11 (NIV)*

Monday, February 13

Then I will give her her vineyards from there, and the valley of Achor as a door of hope. And she will sing there as in the days of her youth, as in the day when she came up from the land of Egypt. *Hosea 2:15 (NASB)*

Tuesday, February 14

Though I have afflicted you, I will afflict you no longer. *Nahum 1:12b (NASB)*

Wednesday, February 15

Woe to [those] who [build] a city with bloodshed and [found] a town with violence! *Habakkuk 2:12 (NASB)*

Thursday, February 16

Behold, God is my salvation, I will trust and not be afraid; for the Lord God is my strength and song, and [God] has become my salvation. *Isaiah 12:2 (NASB)*

Friday, February 17

Do not let my heart be drawn to what is evil so that I take part in wicked deeds along with those who are evildoers; do not let me eat their delicacies. *Psalm 141:4 (NIV)*

Saturday, February 18

Do not fret because of evildoers. Do not envy the wicked. *Proverbs 24:19 (NRSV)*

Week 6: February 19-25, 2017

A society that is based on fear rather than on freedom kills the soul and spirit of its people, along with their capacity for innovation and creativity.

Mitri Raheb
Faith in the Face of Empire (116)

Sunday, February 19

Restore our fortunes, Lord, like streams in the Negev.
Psalm 126:4 (NIV)

Monday, February 20

Now Hazael king of Aram had oppressed Israel all the days of
Jehoahaz. *2 Kings 13:22 (NASB)*

Tuesday, February 21

Grace to you and peace from God the Father and the Lord Jesus
Christ. *2 Thessalonians 1:2 (NASB)*

Wednesday, February 22

If you lend money to My people, to the poor among you, you
are not to act as a creditor to [them]; you shall not charge [them]
interest. *Exodus 22:25 (NASB)*

Thursday, February 23

[God] rules the world in righteousness and judges the peoples with
equity. *Psalm 9:8 (NIV)*

Friday, February 24

The light shines in the darkness, and the darkness did not overcome
it. *John 1:5 (NRSV)*

Saturday, February 25

Grace, mercy and peace from God the Father and Christ Jesus our
Lord. *2 Timothy 1:2 (NASB)*

Week 7: February 26—March 4, 2017

We cannot call a society, a government, or a situation Christian when our brothers and sisters suffer so much in those inveterate and unjust structures.

Oscar A. Romero
The Violence of Love (124)

Sunday, February 26

Ensure your servant's well-being; do not let the arrogant oppress me. *Psalm 119:122 (NIV)*

Monday, February 27

For the land is full of adulterers; for the land mourns because of the curse. The pastures of the wilderness have dried up. Their course also is evil and their might is not right. *Jeremiah 23:10 (NASB)*

Tuesday, February 28

Restore us, O God; make your face shine on us, that we may be saved. *Psalm 80:3 (NIV)*

Wednesday, March 1 - *Ash Wednesday*

Help us, God our Savior, for the glory of your name; deliver us and forgive our sins for your name's sake. *Psalm 79:9 (NIV)*

Thursday, March 2

For You have made a city into a heap, a fortified city into a ruin; a palace of strangers is a city no more, it will never be rebuilt. *Isaiah 25:2 (NASB)*

Friday, March 3

Then he will answer them, "Truly I tell you, just as you did not do it to one of the least of these, you did not do it to me." *Matthew 25:45 (NRSV)*

Saturday, March 4

Hide me from the conspiracy of the wicked, from the plots of evildoers. *Psalm 64:2 (NIV)*

Week 8: March 5-11, 2017

In both the Old and New Testament, the heart of the message is that of love and mercy, justice and peace, liberation and nonviolence, forgiveness and reconciliation. Any message that does not emphasize these and similar characteristics cannot be a message of God to us.

Naim Ateek
The Bible and the Palestine/Israel Conflict (25)

Sunday, March 5

In all their affliction [God] was afflicted, and the angel of [God's] presence saved them; in [God's] love and in [God's] mercy [God] redeemed them, and [God] lifted them and carried them all the days of old. *Isaiah 63:9 (NASB)*

Monday, March 6

For you always have the poor with you, but you do not always have Me. *Matthew 26:11 (NASB)*

Tuesday, March 7

The evil are ensnared by the transgression of their lips, but the righteous escape from trouble. *Proverbs 12:13 (NRSV)*

Wednesday, March 8

Grace to you and peace from God our Father and the Lord Jesus Christ. *Ephesians 1:2 (NASB)*

Thursday, March 9

Your righteousness is like the highest mountains, your justice like the great deep. You, Lord, preserve both people and animals. *Psalm 36:6 (NIV)*

Friday, March 10

Will you keep to the ancient path which wicked men have trod? *Job 22:15 (NASB)*

Saturday, March 11

[God] has redeemed my soul from going down to the Pit, and my life shall see the light. *Job 33:28 (NRSV)*

Week 9: March 12-18, 2017

No one can deny the persisting continuities of long traditions, sustained habitations, national languages, and cultural geographies, but there seems no reason except fear and prejudice to keep insisting on their separation and distinctiveness, as if that was all human life was about.

Edward W. Said

Culture and Imperialism (336)

Sunday, March 12

The righteous hate falsehood, but the wicked act shamefully and disgracefully. *Proverbs 13:5 (NRSV)*

Monday, March 13

I am the Lord your God, who brought you out of the land of Egypt, to give you the land of Canaan, to be your God. *Leviticus 25:38 (NRSV)*

Tuesday, March 14

I was naked and you gave me clothing. *Matthew 25:36a (NRSV)*

Wednesday, March 15

Hear my cry for help, my King and my God, for to you I pray. *Psalm 5:2 (NIV)*

Thursday, March 16

And You save an afflicted people; But Your eyes are on the haughty whom You abase. *2 Samuel 22:28 (NASB)*

Friday, March 17

A poor widow came and put in two small copper coins, which are worth a penny. Then he called his disciples and said to them, "Truly I tell you, this poor widow has put in more than all those who are contributing to the treasury. For all of them have contributed out of their abundance; but she out of her poverty has put in everything she had, all she had to live on." *Mark 12:42-44 (NRSV)*

Saturday, March 18

But strive first for the kingdom of God and his righteousness, and all these things will be given to you as well. *Matthew 6:33 (NRSV)*

Week 10: March 19-25, 2017

Do our resources, power, and relationships and our religion—how we fear God—serve those who are vulnerable and oppressed, the masses of people, not the advantaged or our own personal lives?

Megan McKenna
Not Counting Women and Children (52)

Sunday, March 19

Then hear from heaven and act and judge Your servants, punishing the wicked by bringing [their] way on [their] own heads and justifying the righteous by giving [them] according to [their] righteousness. *2 Chronicles 6:23 (NASB)*

Monday, March 20

Thus says the Lord, "For three transgressions of Israel and for four I will not revoke its punishment, because they sell the righteous for money and the needy for a pair of sandals." *Amos 2:6 (NASB)*

Tuesday, March 21

[God] does not ignore the cries of the afflicted. *Psalm 9:12b (NIV)*

Wednesday, March 22

Blessed are the poor in spirit, for theirs is the kingdom of heaven. *Matthew 5:3 (NRSV)*

Thursday, March 23

[God] raises the poor from the dust and lifts the needy from the ash heap. *Psalm 113:7 (NIV)*

Friday, March 24

It is [God] who sits above the circle of the earth, and its inhabitants are like grasshoppers, who stretches out the heavens like a curtain and spreads them out like a tent to dwell in. [God] it is who reduces rulers to nothing, who makes the judges of the earth meaningless. *Isaiah 40:22-23 (NASB)*

Saturday, March 25

Now it came about in the course of those many days that the king of Egypt died. And the sons of Israel sighed because of the bondage, and they cried out; and their cry for help because of their bondage rose up to God. *Exodus 2:23 (NASB)*

Week 11: March 26—April 1, 2017

Evidence of the presence of the Kingdom of God is thick
wherever and whenever people stand on the promise of God that
there is more to this world—more to this life—than what we see.
There is more than the getting over, getting by, or getting mine.
There is more than the brokenness, the destruction, and the despair
that threaten to wash over us like the waters of the deep. There is
a vision of a world where God cuts through the chaos, where God
speaks and there is light. There is a vision where there is protection
and where love is binding every relationship together.

Lisa Sharon Harper
The Very Good Gospel (205)

Sunday, March 26

The righteous person may have many troubles, but the Lord delivers [them] from them all. *Psalm 34:19 (NIV)*

Monday, March 27

Administer justice every morning. *Jeremiah 21:12a (NASB)*

Tuesday, March 28

Learn to do good; seek justice. *Isaiah 1:17a (NASB)*

Wednesday, March 29

Everyone deceives [their] neighbor and does not speak the truth, they have taught their tongue to speak lies; they weary themselves committing iniquity. *Jeremiah 9:5 (NASB)*

Thursday, March 30

I will restore them because I have compassion on them. They will be as though I had not rejected them, for I am the Lord their God and I will answer them. *Zechariah 10:6b (NIV)*

Friday, March 31

The Lord enters into judgment with the elders and princes of [God's] people, "It is you who have devoured the vineyard; the plunder of the poor is in your houses." *Isaiah 3:14 (NASB)*

Saturday, April 1

On the contrary: "If your enemy is hungry feed him; if he is thirsty, give him something to drink." *Romans 12:20a (NIV)*

Week 12: April 2-8, 2017

Because God is a God of justice, in any situation in which power is misused and the powerful take advantage of the weak, God takes the side of the weak.

C. Rene Padilla
"God's Call to Do Justice,"
in *The Justice Project* (24)

Sunday, April 2

Six days you are to do your work, but on the seventh day you shall cease from labor so that your ox and your donkey may rest, and the son of your female slave, as well as your stranger, may refresh themselves. *Exodus 23:12 (NASB)*

Monday, April 3

When you reap your harvest in your field and have forgotten a sheaf in the field, you shall not go back to get it; it shall be for the alien, for the orphan, and for the widow, in order that the Lord your God may bless you in all the work of your hands. *Deuteronomy 24:19 (NASB)*

Tuesday, April 4

The fruit of the righteous is a tree of life, but violence takes lives away. *Proverbs 11:30 (NRSV)*

Wednesday, April 5

You shall not strip your vineyard bare, or gather the fallen grapes of your vineyard; you shall leave them for the poor and the alien: I am the Lord your God. *Leviticus 19:10 (NRSV)*

Thursday, April 6

But now, Lord, what do I look for? My hope is in you. *Psalm 39:7 (NIV)*

Friday, April 7

For as the earth brings forth its sprouts, and as a garden causes the things sown in it to spring up, so the Lord God will cause righteousness and praise to spring up before all the nations. *Isaiah 61:11 (NASB)*

Saturday, April 8

You shall not reap the aftergrowth of your harvest or gather the grapes of your unpruned vine: it shall be a year of complete rest for the land. *Leviticus 25:5 (NRSV)*

Week 13: April 9-15, 2017

God suffers because God is vulnerable, and God is vulnerable because God loves—and it is love, not suffering or even vulnerability, that is finally the point. God can help because God acts out of love, and love risks suffering.

William C. Placher
Narratives of a Vulnerable God (18)

Sunday, April 9 - *Palm Sunday*

Violence will not be heard again in your land, nor devastation or destruction within your borders; but you will call your walls salvation, and your gates praise. *Isaiah 60:18 (NASB)*

Monday, April 10

One who justifies the wicked and one who condemns the righteous are both alike an abomination to the Lord. *Proverbs 17:15 (NRSV)*

Tuesday, April 11

"But let the one who boasts boast about this: that they have the understanding to know me, that I am the Lord, who exercises kindness, justice and righteousness on earth, for in these I delight," declares the Lord. *Jeremiah 9:24 (NIV)*

Wednesday, April 12

Watch the field where the men are harvesting, and follow along after the women. I have told the men not to lay a hand on you. And whenever you are thirsty, go and get a drink from the water jars the men have filled. *Ruth 2:9 (NIV)*

Thursday, April 13

Hear me, Lord, my plea is just; listen to my cry. Hear my prayer—it does not rise from deceitful lips. *Psalm 17:1 (NIV)*

Friday, April 14 - *Good Friday*

Surely our griefs [Jesus] . . . bore, and our sorrows [Jesus] carried; yet we ourselves esteemed [Jesus] stricken, smitten of God, and afflicted. *Isaiah 53:4 (NASB)*

Saturday, April 15 - *Holy Saturday*

Behold, My Servant, whom I uphold; my chosen one in whom My soul delights. I have put My Spirit upon Him; He will bring forth justice to the nations. *Isaiah 42:1 (NASB)*

Week 14: April 16-22, 2017

The crucified God is in fact a stateless and classless God. But that does not mean that he is an unpolitical God. He is the God of the poor, the oppressed and the humiliated.

Jürgen Moltmann
The Crucified God (329)

Sunday, April 16 - *Easter Sunday*

Then your light will break out like the dawn, and your recovery will speedily spring forth. *Isaiah 58:8a (NASB)*

Monday, April 17

The field of the poor may yield much food, but it is swept away through injustice. *Proverbs 13:23 (NRSV)*

Tuesday, April 18

The Lord's curse is on the house of the wicked, but he blesses the abode of the righteous. *Proverbs 3:33 (NRSV)*

Wednesday, April 19

For this is what the Lord says: "I will extend peace to her like a river, and the wealth of nations like a flooding stream; you will nurse and be carried on her arm and dandled on her knees." *Isaiah 66:12 (NIV)*

Thursday, April 20

And he gave her his hand and raised her up; and calling the saints and widows, he presented her alive. *Acts 9:41 (NASB)*

Friday, April 21

Why do the wicked still live, continue on, also become very powerful? *Job 21:7 (NASB)*

Saturday, April 22

Sustain me, my God, according to your promise, and I will live; do not let my hopes be dashed. *Psalm 119:116 (NIV)*

Week 15: April 23-29, 2017

The light of God is shattering and splintered . . . the light of God illuminates the unjust places of the world in photographic clarity even as it reveals the fragility and loveliness of the human being and humanity's longing for beloved community.

Charles Marsh
The Beloved Community (212)

Sunday, April 23

Endless ruin has overtaken my enemies, you have uprooted their cities; even the memory of them has perished. *Psalm 9:6 (NIV)*

Monday, April 24

"There is no peace for the wicked," says the Lord. *Isaiah 48:22 (NASB)*

Tuesday, April 25

Even in darkness light dawns for the upright, for those who are gracious and compassionate and righteous. *Psalm 112:4 (NIV)*

Wednesday, April 26

They will say of Me, "Only in the Lord are righteousness and strength." Men will come to [God], and all who were angry at [God] will be put to shame. *Isaiah 45:24 (NASB)*

Thursday, April 27

However, if you have warned the righteous man that the righteous should not sin and he does not sin, he shall surely live because he took warning; and you have delivered yourself. *Ezekiel 3:21 (NASB)*

Friday, April 28

She opens her hand to the poor, and reaches out her hands to the needy. *Proverbs 31:20 (NRSV)*

Saturday, April 29

For you will go out with joy and be led forth with peace; the mountains and the hills will break forth into shouts of joy before you, and all the trees of the field will clap their hands. *Isaiah 55:12 (NASB)*

Week 16: April 30—May 6, 2017

Let us rejoice in poverty, because Christ was poor. Let us love to live with the poor, because they are specially loved by Christ. Even the lowest, most depraved—we must see Christ in them and love them to folly. When we suffer from dirt, lack of privacy, heat and cold, coarse food, let us rejoice.

Dorothy Day
On Pilgrimage (250)

Sunday, April 30

The light of the righteous rejoices, but the lamp of the wicked goes out. *Proverbs 13:9 (NRSV)*

Monday, May 1

With God we will gain the victory, and [God] will trample down our enemies. *Psalm 60:12 (NIV)*

Tuesday, May 2

Do not swerve to the right or to the left; turn your foot away from evil. *Proverbs 4:27 (NRSV)*

Wednesday, May 3

The poor use entreaties, but the rich answer roughly. *Proverbs 18:23 (NRSV)*

Thursday, May 4

Blessed are you when people revile you and persecute you and utter all kinds of evil against you falsely on my account. Rejoice and be glad, for your reward is great in heaven, for in the same way they persecuted the prophets who were before you. *Matthew 5:11-12 (NRSV)*

Friday, May 5

This is what the wicked are like—always free of care, they go on amassing wealth. *Psalm 73:12 (NIV)*

Saturday, May 6

[Love] bears all things, believes all things, hopes all things, endures all things. *1 Corinthians 13:7 (NASB)*

Week 17: May 7-13, 2017

[We are] not to just bandage the victims under the wheel, but to jam a spoke in the wheel itself.

Dietrich Bonhoeffer
A Testament of Freedom (139)

Sunday, May 7

The rich and the poor have this in common: the Lord is the maker of them all. *Proverbs 22:2 (NRSV)*

Monday, May 8

Keep far from a false charge, and do not kill the innocent or the righteous, for I will not acquit the guilty. *Exodus 23:7 (NASB)*

Tuesday, May 9

When I say to the righteous he will surely live, and he so trusts in his righteousness that he commits iniquity, none of his righteous deeds will be remembered; but in that same iniquity of his which he has committed he will die. *Ezekiel 33:13 (NASB)*

Wednesday, May 10

"Peace, peace to [those] who [are] far and to [those] who [are] near," says the Lord, "and I will heal [them]." *Isaiah 57:19b (NASB)*

Thursday, May 11

For the brokenness of the daughter of my people I am broken; I mourn, dismay has taken hold of me. *Jeremiah 8:21 (NASB)*

Friday, May 12

The Spirit and the bride say, "Come!" And let the one who hears say, "Come!" Let the one who is thirsty come; and let the one who wishes take the free gift of the water of life. *Revelation 22:17 (NIV)*

Saturday, May 13

For it is not those who hear the law who are righteous in God's sight, but it is those who obey the law who will be declared righteous. *Romans 2:13 (NIV)*

Week 18: May 14-20, 2017

The unavoidable reality is that, by the year 2050, projections point to a nation without an ethnic majority. America will no longer be a Eurocentric, white nation. Furthermore, as previously stated, the nonwhite population among Christians is growing faster than in the general population. American Christianity will become nonwhite before the rest of American society.

Soong-Chan Rah
The Next Evangelicalism (74)

Sunday, May 14

If you return to the Almighty, you will be restored; if you remove unrighteousness far from your tent. *Job 22:23 (NASB)*

Monday, May 15

Blessed are you when people hate you, and when they exclude you, revile you, and defame you on account of the Son of Man. *Luke 6:22 (NRSV)*

Tuesday, May 16

Bless those who curse you, pray for those who mistreat you. *Luke 6:28 (NASB)*

Wednesday, May 17

Then they cried to the Lord in their trouble, and [God] brought them out from their distress. *Psalm 107.28 (NRSV)*

Thursday, May 18

However, there will be no poor among you, since the Lord will surely bless you in the land which the Lord your God is giving you as an inheritance to possess. *Deuteronomy 15:4 (NASB)*

Friday, May 19

You shall remember that you were a slave in the land of Egypt; therefore I am commanding you to do this thing. *Deuteronomy 24:22 (NASB)*

Saturday, May 20

"Because the poor are plundered and the needy groan, I will now arise," says the Lord. "I will protect them from those who malign them." *Psalm 12:5 (NIV)*

Week 19: May 21-27, 2017

We hope for the sake of the broken world. We hope that the world may be healed and made whole. The hope that reaches to us from the future is a hope born in the past in the event of the cross and resurrection.

Charles Marsh
The Beloved Community (212)

Sunday, May 21

Your righteousness is everlasting and your law is true.
Psalm 119:142 (NIV)

Monday, May 22

Do not oppress the widow or the fatherless, the foreigner or the
poor. *Zechariah 7:10a (NIV)*

Tuesday, May 23

Zacchaeus stood there and said to the Lord, "Look, half of my
possessions, Lord, I will give to the poor; and if I have defrauded
anyone of anything, I will pay back four times as much."
Luke 19:8 (NRSV)

Wednesday, May 24

Whoever is kind to the poor lends to the Lord, and will be repaid in
full. *Proverbs 19:17 (NRSV)*

Thursday, May 25

For the company of the godless is barren, and fire consumes the
tents of the corrupt. *Job 15:34 (NASB)*

Friday, May 26

Grace, mercy and peace from God the Father and Christ Jesus our
Lord. *1 Timothy 1:2 (NASB)*

Saturday, May 27

Do not rob the poor because they are poor, or crush the afflicted at
the gate. *Proverbs 22:22 (NRSV)*

Week 20: May 28—June 3, 2017

The mystery of poverty is that by sharing in it, making ourselves poor in giving to others, we increase our knowledge of and belief in love.

Dorothy Day
The Catholic Worker

Sunday, May 28

Do not grant the wicked their desires, Lord; do not let their plans succeed. *Psalm 140:8 (NIV)*

Monday, May 29 - *Memorial Day*

Remember the prisoners, as though in prison with them, and those who are ill-treated, since you yourselves also are in the body. *Hebrews 13:3 (NASB)*

Tuesday, May 30

The Lord will vindicate me; your love, Lord, endures forever—do not abandon the works of your hands. *Psalm 138:8 (NIV)*

Wednesday, May 31

I walk in the way of righteousness, along the paths of justice. *Proverbs 8:20 (NRSV)*

Thursday, June 1

Now she who is a widow indeed and who has been left alone, has fixed her hope on God and continues in entreaties and prayers night and day. *1 Timothy 5:5 (NASB)*

Friday, June 2

He who supplies seed to the sower and bread for food will supply and multiply your seed for sowing and increase the harvest of your righteousness. *2 Corinthians 9:10 (NASB)*

Saturday, June 3

"Behold, I am going to deal at that time with all your oppressors." *Zephaniah 3:19a (NASB)*

Week 21: June 4-10, 2017

"Realism" is the language of the demonic whose purpose is to seduce us into believing that we have no other choice.

Darrell J. Fasching
Narrative Theology After Auschwitz (147)

Sunday, June 4 - *Pentecost Sunday*

For I will pour out water on the thirsty land and streams on the dry ground; I will pour out My Spirit on your offspring and My blessing on your descendants. *Isaiah 44:3 (NASB)*

Monday, June 5

He has seized a house which he has not built. *Job 20:19b (NASB)*

Tuesday, June 6

Then I charged your judges at that time, saying, "Hear the cases between your fellow countrymen, and judge righteously between a man and his fellow countryman, or the alien who is with him." *Deuteronomy 1:16 (NASB)*

Wednesday, June 7

Bring to an end the violence of the wicked and make the righteous secure—you, the righteous God who probes minds and hearts. *Psalm 7:9 (NIV)*

Thursday, June 8

Will not all of these take up a taunt-song against him, even mockery and insinuations against him and say, "Woe to him who increases what is not his— for how long—and makes himself rich with loans?" *Habakkuk 2:6 (NASB)*

Friday, June 9

Do not wear yourself out to get rich; be wise enough to desist. *Proverbs 23:4 (NRSV)*

Saturday, June 10

Why do you hide your face and forget our misery and oppression? *Psalm 44:24 (NIV)*

Week 22: June 11-17, 2017

America must re-examine old presuppositions and release itself from many things that for centuries have been held sacred. For the evils of racism, poverty and militarism to die, a new set of values must be born.

Martin Luther King, Jr.
Where Do We Go from Here:
Chaos or Community? (133)

Sunday, June 11

Where will you be stricken again, as you continue in your rebellion? The whole head is sick and the whole heart is faint. *Isaiah 1:5 (NASB)*

Monday, June 12

Let the peace of Christ rule in your hearts, to which indeed you were called in one body; and be thankful. *Colossians 3:15 (NASB)*

Tuesday, June 13

Behold, as for the proud one, [their] soul is not right within [them]; but the righteous will live by [their] faith. *Habakkuk 2:4 (NASB)*

Wednesday, June 14

I am a stranger and a sojourner among you; give me a burial site among you that I may bury my dead out of my sight. *Genesis 23:4 (NASB)*

Thursday, June 15

Then He said to me, "The iniquity of the house of Israel and Judah is very, very great, and the land is filled with blood and the city is full of perversion; for they say, 'The Lord has forsaken the land, and the Lord does not see!'" *Ezekiel 9:9 (NASB)*

Friday, June 16

But I say to you, "Love your enemies and pray for those who persecute you." *Matthew 5:44 (NRSV)*

Saturday, June 17

On that day the deaf will hear words of a book, and out of their gloom and darkness the eyes of the blind will see. *Isaiah 29:18 (NASB)*

Week 23: June 18-24, 2017

What is at stake is the credibility and promise of the Christian gospel and the hope that we may heal the wounds of racial violence that continue to divide our churches and our society.

James H. Cone
The Cross and the Lynching Tree (xiii-xiv)

Sunday, June 18

They do not speak peaceably, but devise false accusations against those who live quietly in the land. *Psalm 35:20 (NIV)*

Monday, June 19

They will beat their swords into plowshares and their spears into pruning hooks. *Micah 4:3b (NIV)*

Tuesday, June 20

In my distress I called upon the Lord, yes, I cried to my God; and from [God's] temple [God] heard my voice, and my cry for help came into [God's] ears. *2 Samuel 22:7 (NASB)*

Wednesday, June 21

Grace, mercy and peace will be with us, from God the Father and from Jesus Christ, the Son of the Father, in truth and love. *2 John 1:3 (NASB)*

Thursday, June 22

On the following day, when they came from Bethany, he was hungry. *Mark 11:12 (NRSV)*

Friday, June 23

The Lord works vindication and justice for all who are oppressed. *Psalm 103:6 (NRSV)*

Saturday, June 24

All of us growl like bears, and moan sadly like doves; we hope for justice, but there is none, for salvation, but it is far from us. *Isaiah 59:11 (NASB)*

Week 24: June 25—July 1, 2017

People do not get crucified for charity. People are crucified for living out a love that disrupts the social order, that calls forth a new world. People are not crucified for helping poor people. People are crucified for joining them.

Shane Claiborne
The Irresistible Revolution (129)

Sunday, June 25

That Your eyes may be open to the supplication of Your servant and to the supplication of Your people Israel, to listen to them whenever they call to You. *I Kings 8:52 (NASB)*

Monday, June 26

Those who rebuke the wicked will have delight, and a good blessing will come upon them. *Proverbs 24:25 (NRSV)*

Tuesday, June 27

My eyes fail, looking for your salvation, looking for your righteous promise. *Psalm 119:123 (NIV)*

Wednesday, June 28

The Lord loves righteousness and justice; the earth is full of his unfailing love. *Psalm 33:5 (NIV)*

Thursday, June 29

Arise, O Lord; O God, lift up Your hand. Do not forget the afflicted. *Psalm 10:12 (NASB)*

Friday, June 30

I have said this to you, so that in me you may have peace. In the world you face persecution. But take courage; I have conquered the world! *John 16:33 (NRSV)*

Saturday, July 1

The tongue of the righteous is choice silver; the mind of the wicked is of little worth. *Proverbs 10:20 (NRSV)*

Week 25: July 2-8, 2017

The institution of race broke America at its foundations. It will not be enough to tinker here and there. We need to envision a new way of being together. Fundamentally, this will mean the interrogation of all our assumptions about how our society should be. It will mean imagining a world where everyone—especially the least of these—has enough to thrive.

Lisa Sharon Harper
The Very Good Gospel (157)

Sunday, July 2

But the Lord is righteous; he has cut me free from the cords of the wicked. *Psalm 129:4 (NIV)*

Monday, July 3

In reply he said to them, "Whoever has two coats must share with anyone who has none; and whoever has food must do likewise." *Luke 3:11 (NRSV)*

Tuesday, July 4 - *Independence Day*

Open the gates, that the righteous nation may enter, the one that remains faithful. *Isaiah 26:2 (NASB)*

Wednesday, July 5

Hear my cry, O God; listen to my prayer. *Psalm 61:1 (NIV)*

Thursday, July 6

The unjust are an abomination to the righteous, but the upright are an abomination to the wicked. *Proverbs 29:27 (NRSV)*

Friday, July 7

[The Lord] sent out his word and healed them, and delivered them from destruction. *Psalm 107:20 (NRSV)*

Saturday, July 8

You exalted me above my foes; from a violent man you rescued me. *Psalm 18:48b (NIV)*

Week 26: July 9-15, 2017

True mercy, the mercy God gives to us and teaches us, demands justice.

Pope Francis
The Church of Mercy (107)

Sunday, July 9

The Levite, because he has no portion or inheritance among you, and the alien, the orphan and the widow who are in your town, shall come and eat and be satisfied, in order that the Lord your God may bless you in all the work of your hand which you do. *Deuteronomy 14:29 (NASB)*

Monday, July 10

May there be peace within your walls and security within your citadels. *Psalm 122:7 (NIV)*

Tuesday, July 11

Do not enter the path of the wicked, and do not walk in the way of evildoers. *Proverbs 4:14 (NRSV)*

Wednesday, July 12

If only you had paid attention to My commandments! Then your well-being would have been like a river, and your righteousness like the waves of the sea. *Isaiah 48:18 (NASB)*

Thursday, July 13

And he answered them, "Go and tell John what you have seen and heard: the blind receive their sight, the lame walk, the lepers are cleansed, the deaf hear, the dead are raised, the poor have good news brought to them." *Luke 7:22 (NRSV)*

Friday, July 14

Return to your fortress, you prisoners of hope; even now I announce that I will restore twice as much to you. *Zechariah 9:12 (NIV)*

Saturday, July 15

The stranger has not lodged in the street; I have opened my doors to the traveler. *Job 31:32 (NRSV)*

Week 27: July 16-22, 2017

We'll practice the ways of Jesus, over and over, until the scales fall from our eyes and our ears begin to hear.

Sarah Bessey
Jesus Feminist (6)

Sunday, July 16

Now may the Lord of peace Himself continually grant
you peace in every circumstance. The Lord be with you all!
2 Thessalonians 3:16 (NASB)

Monday, July 17

Deliver me from evildoers and save me from those who are after my
blood. *Psalm 59:2 (NIV)*

Tuesday, July 18

Foreigners will build up your walls, and their kings will minister
to you; for in My wrath I struck you, and in My favor I have had
compassion on you. *Isaiah 60:10 (NASB)*

Wednesday, July 19

Do not plot evil against each other. *Zechariah 7:10b (NIV)*

Thursday, July 20

Let me hear joy and gladness; let the bones you have crushed rejoice.
Psalm 51:8 (NIV)

Friday, July 21

The perverse get what their ways deserve, and the good, what their
deeds deserve. *Proverbs 14:14 (NRSV)*

Saturday, July 22

The Lord is known by his acts of justice; the wicked are ensnared by
the work of their hands. *Psalm 9:16 (NIV)*

Week 28: July 23-29, 2017

The authentic community of saints is bound up with the encounter of God in the midst of a broken existence, struggling to be free.

James H. Cone
The Spirituals and the Blues (60)

Sunday, July 23

It was revoked on that day, and so the oppressed of the flock who were watching me knew it was the word of the Lord. *Zechariah 11:11 (NIV)*

Monday, July 24

So you shall know that I, the Lord your God, dwell in Zion, my holy mountain. And Jerusalem shall be holy, and strangers shall never again pass through it. *Joel 3:17 (NRSV)*

Tuesday, July 25

We have become orphans, fatherless; our mothers are like widows. *Lamentations 5:3 (NRSV)*

Wednesday, July 26

But as for you, brethren, do not grow weary of doing good. *2 Thessalonians 3:13 (NASB)*

Thursday, July 27

Remove far from me falsehood and lying; give me neither poverty nor riches; feed me with the food that I need. *Proverbs 30:8 (NRSV)*

Friday, July 28

This poor soul cried, and was heard by the Lord, and was saved from every trouble. *Psalms 34:6 (NRSV)*

Saturday, July 29

Do not say, "I will do to others as they have done to me; I will pay them back for what they have done." *Proverbs 24:29 (NRSV)*

Week 29: July 30—August 5, 2017

Peace is built with every small and large act of forgiveness.

Desmond and Mpho Tutu
The Book of Forgiving (59)

Sunday, July 30

Do not shed innocent blood in this place. *Jeremiah 22:3d (NASB)*

Monday, July 31

Restore us again, God our Savior, and put away your displeasure toward us. *Psalm 85:4 (NIV)*

Tuesday, August 1

And I said: Listen, you heads of Jacob and rulers of the house of Israel! Should you not know justice? *Micah 3:1 (NRSV)*

Wednesday, August 2

Continue your love to those who know you, your righteousness to the upright in heart. *Psalm 36:10 (NIV)*

Thursday, August 3

Save me, O God, by your name; vindicate me by your might. *Psalm 54:1 (NIV)*

Friday, August 4

In you, Lord, I have taken refuge; let me never be put to shame; deliver me in your righteousness. *Psalm 31:1 (NIV)*

Saturday, August 5

Happy are those who observe justice, who do righteousness at all times. *Psalm 106:3 (NRSV)*

Week 30: August 6-12, 2017

The kingdom of God points to an inverted, or upside down, way of life that contrasts with the prevailing social order. . . . Kingdom values challenge patterns of social life taken for granted in modern culture.

Donald B. Kraybill
The Upside-Down Kingdom (19)

Sunday, August 6

They have treated father and mother lightly within you. The alien they have oppressed in your midst; the fatherless and the widow they have wronged in you. *Ezekiel 22:7 (NASB)*

Monday, August 7

The Lord has made his salvation known and revealed his righteousness to the nations. *Psalm 98:2 (NIV)*

Tuesday, August 8

For behold what earnestness this very thing, this godly sorrow, has produced in you: what vindication of yourselves, what indignation, what fear, what longing, what zeal, what avenging of wrong! In everything you demonstrated yourselves to be innocent in the matter. *2 Corinthians 7:11 (NASB)*

Wednesday, August 9

But if we are afflicted, it is for your comfort and salvation; or if we are comforted, it is for your comfort. *2 Corinthians 1:6a (NASB)*

Thursday, August 10

It will be as when a hungry man dreams—and behold, he is eating; but when he awakens, his hunger is not satisfied, or as when a thirsty man dreams—and behold, he is drinking, but when he awakens, behold, he is faint and his thirst is not quenched. Thus the multitude of all the nations will be who wage war against Mount Zion. *Isaiah 29:8 (NASB)*

Friday, August 11

[I was] sick and in prison and you did not visit me. *Matthew 25:43c (NRSV)*

Saturday, August 12

The Lord is gracious and righteous; our God is full of compassion. *Psalm 116:5 (NIV)*

Week 31: August 13-19, 2017

In the final analysis, the rich must not ignore the poor because both rich and poor are tied together.

Martin Luther King, Jr.
Where Do We Go from Here:
Chaos or Community? (180)

Sunday, August 13

Too long have I lived among those who hate peace.
Psalm 120:6 (NIV)

Monday, August 14

The thoughts of the righteous are just; the advice of the wicked is treacherous. *Proverbs 12:5 (NRSV)*

Tuesday, August 15

Many seek the favor of a ruler, but it is from the Lord that one gets justice. *Proverbs 29:26 (NRSV)*

Wednesday, August 16

At that time Jesus went through the grainfields on the sabbath; his disciples were hungry, and they began to pluck heads of grain and to eat. *Matthew 12:1 (NRSV)*

Thursday, August 17

A people whom you do not know shall eat up the produce of your ground and all your labors, and you will never be anything but oppressed and crushed continually. *Deuteronomy 28:33 (NASB)*

Friday, August 18

Therefore the law is ignored and justice is never upheld. For the wicked surround the righteous; therefore justice comes out perverted. *Habakkuk 1:4 (NASB)*

Saturday, August 19

But the Lord your God you shall fear; and [God] will deliver you from the hand of all your enemies. *2 Kings 17:39 (NASB)*

Week 32: August 20-26, 2017

Let gratitude and the humility of participation shape our devotion to life.

Charles Marsh
The Beloved Community (213)

Sunday, August 20

The Lord is righteous . . . and kind. Psalm 145:17 (NASB)

Monday, August 21

Be assured, the wicked will not go unpunished, but those who are righteous will escape. *Proverbs 11:21 (NRSV)*

Tuesday, August 22

That fiftieth year shall be a jubilee for you: you shall not sow, or reap the aftergrowth, or harvest the unpruned vines. *Leviticus 25:11 (NRSV)*

Wednesday, August 23

Also the foreigners who join themselves to the Lord, to minister to Him, and to love the name of the Lord, to be His servants, every one who keeps from profaning the sabbath and holds fast My covenant. *Isaiah 56:6 (NASB)*

Thursday, August 24

For we rejoice when we ourselves are weak but you are strong; this we also pray for, that you be made complete. *2 Corinthians 13:9 (NASB)*

Friday, August 25

"The latter glory of this house will be greater than the former," says the Lord of hosts, "and in this place I will give peace," declares the Lord of hosts. *Haggai 2:9 (NASB)*

Saturday, August 26

The steadfast love of the Lord is from everlasting to everlasting on those who fear him, and his righteousness to children's children. *Psalm 103:17 (NRSV)*

Week 33: August 27—September 2, 2017

The common good will not be attained by excluding people. We can't enrich the common good of our country by driving out those we don't care for. We have to try to bring out all that is good in each person and try to develop an atmosphere of trust, not with physical force, as though dealing with irrational beings, but with a moral force that draws out the good that is in everyone.

Oscar A. Romero
The Violence of Love (3)

Sunday, August 27

Now flee from youthful lusts and pursue righteousness, faith, love and peace, with those who call on the Lord from a pure heart. *2 Timothy 2:22 (NASB)*

Monday, August 28

Grace to you and peace from God our Father. *Colossians 1:2b (NASB)*

Tuesday, August 29

Their children also will be as formerly, and their congregation shall be established before Me; and I will punish all their oppressors. *Jeremiah 30:20 (NASB)*

Wednesday, August 30

Your little ones, your wives, and the alien who is within your camps, from the one who chops your wood to the one who draws your water. *Deuteronomy 29:11 (NASB)*

Thursday, August 31

The Lord therefore be judge and decide between you and me; and may He see and plead my cause and deliver me from your hand. *I Samuel 24:15 (NASB)*

Friday, September 1

The simple believe everything, but the clever consider their steps. *Proverbs 14:15 (NRSV)*

Saturday, September 2

For because of your trust in your own achievements and treasures, even you yourself will be captured; and Chemosh will go off into exile together with his priests and his princes. *Jeremiah 48:7 (NASB)*

Week 34: September 3-9, 2017

Do we believe that the poor have a message for us? When we fail to listen, to see what we can learn, we are in fact telling them that they are without useful information, without contribution. By dismissing what they know, we further mar the identity of the poor. Our good intentions deepen the poverty we seek to alleviate.

Bryant L. Myers
Walking with the Poor (214)

Sunday, September 3

From the city men groan, and the souls of the wounded cry out; yet God does not pay attention to folly. *Job 24:12a (NASB)*

Monday, September 4 - *Labor Day*

You shall remember that you were a slave in the land of Egypt, and the Lord your God brought you out of there by a mighty hand and by an outstretched arm; therefore the Lord your God commanded you to observe the sabbath day. *Deuteronomy 5:15 (NASB)*

Tuesday, September 5

So as to buy the helpless for money and the needy for a pair of sandals, and that we may sell the refuse of the wheat? *Amos 8:6 (NASB)*

Wednesday, September 6

You shall not covet your neighbor's house; you shall not covet your neighbor's wife or his male servant or his female servant or his ox or his donkey or anything that belongs to your neighbor. *Exodus 20:17 (NASB)*

Thursday, September 7

Diverse weights and diverse measures are both alike an abomination to the Lord. *Proverbs 20:10 (NRSV)*

Friday, September 8

Each of them will sit under his vine and under his fig tree, with no one to make them afraid. *Micah 4:4a (NASB)*

Saturday, September 9

But if God so clothes the grass of the field, which is alive today and tomorrow is thrown into the oven, will he not much more clothe you—you of little faith? *Matthew 6:30 (NRSV)*

Week 35: September 10-16, 2017

Embracing our brokenness creates a need and a desire for mercy and perhaps a corresponding need to show mercy.

Bryan Stevenson
Just Mercy: A Story of
Justice and Redemption (290)

Sunday, September 10

Open to me the gates of righteousness; I shall enter through them, I shall give thanks to the Lord. *Psalm 118:19 (NIV)*

Monday, September 11

And I will grant peace in the land, and you shall lie down, and no one shall make you afraid; I will remove dangerous animals from the land, and no sword shall go through your land. *Leviticus 26:6 (NRSV)*

Tuesday, September 12

Truly he is my rock and my salvation; he is my fortress, I will never be shaken. *Psalm 62:2 (NIV)*

Wednesday, September 13

Defend the orphan. *Isaiah 1:17d (NASB)*

Thursday, September 14

Glorious and majestic are his deeds, and his righteousness endures forever. *Psalm 111:3 (NIV)*

Friday, September 15

He enters into peace; they rest in their beds, each one who walked in his upright way. *Isaiah 57:2 (NASB)*

Saturday, September 16

What the wicked dread will come upon them, but the desire of the righteous will be granted. *Proverbs 10:24 (NRSV)*

Week 36: September 17-23, 2017

The biggest problem with America's idea of racial categories is that they're not just categories: they've been used to imply a hierarchy born of nature. Regardless of how racial categories came into being, Americans have been cast in racial roles that have the power to become self-fulfilling, self-perpetuating prophecies.

Debby Irving
*Waking Up White
and Finding Myself in the Story of Race* (41)

Sunday, September 17

Sanctify a fast, call a solemn assembly. Gather the elders and all the inhabitants of the land to the house of the Lord your God, and cry out to the Lord. *Joel 1:14 (NRSV)*

Monday, September 18

They have made their paths crooked, whoever treads on them does not know peace. *Isaiah 59:8b (NASB)*

Tuesday, September 19

Teach me your way, Lord; lead me in a straight path because of my oppressors. *Psalm 27:11 (NIV)*

Wednesday, September 20

I am not at ease, nor am I quiet; I have no rest; but trouble comes. *Job 3:26 (NRSV)*

Thursday, September 21

I abhor the assembly of evildoers and refuse to sit with the wicked. *Psalm 26:5 (NIV)*

Friday, September 22

The Lord delights in those who fear him, who put their hope in his unfailing love. *Psalm 147:11 (NIV)*

Saturday, September 23

[The Lord] will surely be gracious to you at the sound of your cry; when [the Lord] hears it, [the Lord] will answer you. *Isaiah 30:19b (NASB)*

Week 37: September 24-30, 2017

Our patriotism has become a cult of self-worship consecrated by court prophets robed in pinstriped suits. Forgetting the difference between discipleship and patriotism, the God most Americans trust is a simulacrum of the holy and transcendent God, a reification of the American way of life.

Charles Marsh
The Beloved Community (7)

Sunday, September 24

So as to deprive the needy of justice and rob the poor of My people of their rights, so that widows may be their spoil and that they may plunder the orphans. *Isaiah 10:2 (NASB)*

Monday, September 25

The mouth of the righteous brings forth wisdom, but the perverse tongue will be cut off. *Proverbs 10:31 (NRSV)*

Tuesday, September 26

I hate your new moon festivals and your appointed feasts, they have become a burden to Me; I am weary of bearing them. *Isaiah 1:14 (NASB)*

Wednesday, September 27

Is anyone among you suffering? Then [they] must pray. Is anyone cheerful? [They are] to sing praises. *James 5:13 (NASB)*

Thursday, September 28

The Lord hears the needy and does not despise his captive people. *Psalm 69:33 (NIV)*

Friday, September 29

Behold, then, I smite My hand at your dishonest gain which you have acquired and at the bloodshed which is among you. *Ezekiel 22:13 (NASB)*

Saturday, September 30

If I have rejected the cause of my male or female slaves, when they brought a complaint against me; what then shall I do when God rises up? *Job 31:13-14 (NRSV)*

Week 38: October 1-7, 2017

The first step toward love is a common sharing of mutual worth and value.

Howard Thurman
Jesus and the Disinherited (88)

Sunday, October 1

Share with the Lord's people who are in need. Practice hospitality. *Romans 12:13 (NIV)*

Monday, October 2

Whoever sows injustice will reap calamity, and the rod of anger will fail. *Proverbs 22:8 (NRSV)*

Tuesday, October 3

I cry aloud to the Lord; I lift up my voice to the Lord for mercy. *Psalm 142:1 (NIV)*

Wednesday, October 4

The steadfast of mind You will keep in perfect peace, because [they trust] in You. *Isaiah 26:3 (NASB)*

Thursday, October 5

Look on my suffering and deliver me, for I have not forgotten your law. *Psalm 119:153 (NIV)*

Friday, October 6

Now may our Lord Jesus Christ Himself and
God our Father, who [have] loved us and given
us eternal comfort and good hope by grace. . .
2 Thessalonians 2:16 (NASB)

Saturday, October 7

Then my people will live in a peaceful habitation, and in secure dwellings and in undisturbed resting places. *Isaiah 32:18 (NASB)*

Week 39: October 8-14, 2017

Although white southerners lost the Civil War, they did not lose the cultural war—the struggle to define America as a white nation and blacks as a subordinate race unfit for governing and therefore incapable of political and social equality.

James H. Cone
The Cross and the Lynching Tree (6)

Sunday, October 8

You went forth for the salvation of Your people, for the salvation of Your anointed. you struck the head of the house of the evil to lay him open from thigh to neck. *Habakkuk 3:13 (NASB)*

Monday, October 9

Then He said to me, "Son of man, these bones are the whole house of Israel; behold, they say, 'Our bones are dried up and our hope has perished. We are completely cut off.'" *Ezekiel 37:11 (NASB)*

Tuesday, October 10

They will receive blessing from the Lord and vindication from God their Savior. *Psalm 24:5 (NIV)*

Wednesday, October 11

Why, my soul, are you downcast? Why so disturbed within me? Put your hope in God, for I will yet praise him, my Savior and my God. *Psalm 42:5 (NIV)*

Thursday, October 12

He says, "It is too small a thing that You should be My Servant to raise up the tribes of Jacob and to restore the preserved ones of Israel; I will also make You a light of the nations so that My salvation may reach to the end of the earth." *Isaiah 49:6 (NASB)*

Friday, October 13

[The righteous one] does not oppress anyone, but restores to the debtor [their] pledge. *Ezekiel 18:7a (NASB)*

Saturday, October 14

The righteous will rejoice in the Lord and take refuge in [God]; all the upright in heart will glory in [the Lord]! *Psalm 64:10 (NIV)*

Week 40: October 15-21, 2017

The church must be a sample of the kind of humanity within which, for example, economic and racial differences are surmounted. Only then will it have anything to say to the society that surrounds it about how those differences must be dealt with. Otherwise preaching to the world a standard of reconciliation which is not its own experience will be neither honest nor effective.

John Howard Yoder
The Politics of Jesus (150-151)

Sunday, October 15

When the wicked prevail, people go into hiding; but when they perish, the righteous increase. *Proverbs 28:28 (NRSV)*

Monday, October 16

The God of peace be with you all. *Romans 15:33 (NIV)*

Tuesday, October 17

[The children of the foolish] are far from safety, they are crushed in the gate, and there is no one to deliver them. *Job 5:4 (NRSV)*

Wednesday, October 18

But those who suffer he delivers in their suffering; he speaks to them in their affliction. *Job 36:15 (NIV)*

Thursday, October 19

Beware of practicing your piety before others in order to be seen by them; for then you have no reward from your Father in heaven. *Matthew 6:1 (NRSV)*

Friday, October 20

They do not defend the orphan, nor does the widow's plea come before them. *Isaiah 1:23b (NASB)*

Saturday, October 21

Sing joyfully to the Lord, you righteous; it is fitting for the upright to praise him. *Psalm 33:1 (NIV)*

Week 41: October 22-28, 2017

Christ comes not in the form of those who visit the imprisoned but in the imprisoned being cared for.

Nadia Bolz-Weber
Accidental Saints (47)

Sunday, October 22

If you close your ear to the cry of the poor, you will cry out and not be heard. *Proverbs 21:13 (NRSV)*

Monday, October 23

Then they cried to the Lord in their trouble, and he saved them from their distress. *Psalm 107:13 (NIV)*

Tuesday, October 24

Do you not know? Have you not heard? The Everlasting God, the Lord, the Creator of the ends of the earth does not become weary or tired. His understanding is inscrutable. *Isaiah 40:28 (NASB)*

Wednesday, October 25

Others snatch the orphan from the breast, and against the poor they take a pledge. *Job 24:9 (NASB)*

Thursday, October 26

I will seek the lost, bring back the scattered, bind up the broken and strengthen the sick; but the fat and the strong I will destroy. I will feed them with judgment. *Ezekiel 34:16 (NASB)*

Friday, October 27

Boaz commanded his servants, saying, "Let her glean even among the sheaves, and do not insult her. Also you shall purposely pull out for her some grain from the bundles and leave it that she may glean, and do not rebuke her." *Ruth 2:15-16 (NASB)*

Saturday, October 28

Therefore I completely despaired of all the fruit of my labor for which I had labored under the sun. *Ecclesiastes 2:20 (NASB)*

Week 42: October 29—November 4, 2017

Where there is despair, there is now hope. Where there was oppression, there is now opportunity. Where there was defeat, there is now purpose. And where there was weakness, there is now strength—that comes only from God. I face the future buoyant in the courage and confidence born of faith in Jesus Christ alone.

John M. Perkins
Let Justice Roll Down (204-205)

Sunday, October 29

Thus says the Lord of hosts, "The sons of Israel are oppressed, and the sons of Judah as well; and all who took them captive have held them fast, they have refused to let them go." *Jeremiah 50:33 (NASB)*

Monday, October 30

Therefore you will joyously draw water from the springs of salvation. *Isaiah 12:3 (NASB)*

Tuesday, October 31

But if [they are] poor and cannot afford so much, [they] shall take one male lamb for a guilt offering to be elevated, to make atonement on [their] behalf, and one-tenth of an ephah of choice flour mixed with oil for a grain offering and a log of oil. *Leviticus 14:21 (NRSV)*

Wednesday, November 1

But the captain of the guard left some of the poorest of the land to be vinedressers and plowmen. *2 Kings 25:12 (NASB)*

Thursday, November 2

For you have upheld my right and my cause, sitting enthroned as the righteous judge. *Psalm 9:4 (NIV)*

Friday, November 3

Those who devise wicked schemes are near, but they are far from your law. *Psalm 119:150 (NIV)*

Saturday, November 4

You shall remember that you were a slave in the land of Egypt, and the Lord your God redeemed you; therefore I command you this today. *Deuteronomy 15:15 (NASB)*

Week 43: November 5-11, 2017

Patriarchy is not God's dream for humanity.

Sarah Bessey
Jesus Feminist (14)

Sunday, November 5

For the eyes of the Lord are toward the righteous, And His ears attend to their prayer, but the face of the Lord is against those who do evil. *I Peter 3:12 (NASB)*

Monday, November 6

To the weary you have given no water to drink, and from the hungry you have withheld bread. But the earth belongs to the mighty . . . and the honorable [dwell] in it. *Job 22:7-8 (NASB)*

Tuesday, November 7 - *Election Day*

Do you rulers indeed speak justly? Do you judge people with equity? *Psalm 58:1 (NIV)*

Wednesday, November 8

In the Law it is written, "By men of strange tongues and by the lips of strangers I will speak to this people, and even so they will not listen to Me," says the Lord. *1 Corinthians 14:21 (NASB)*

Thursday, November 9

Let the earth open up and salvation bear fruit, and righteousness spring up with it. I, the Lord, have created it. *Isaiah 45:8b (NASB)*

Friday, November 10

Arrogant foes are attacking me, O God; ruthless people are trying to kill me—they have no regard for you. *Psalm 86:14 (NIV)*

Saturday, November 11

Hear me, Lord, and answer me, for I am poor and needy. *Psalm 86:1 (NIV)*

Week 44: November 12-18, 2017

The net result of the fall on the economic, political, and religious systems is that they become the places where people learn to play god in the lives of the poor and the marginalized. When fallen human beings play god in the lives of others, the results are patterns of domination and oppression that mar the image and potential productivity of the poor while alienating the non-poor from their true identity and vocation as well.

Bryant L. Myers
Walking with the Poor (67)

Sunday, November 12

Defend the weak and the fatherless; uphold the cause of the poor and the oppressed. *Psalm 82:3 (NIV)*

Monday, November 13

If any of your kin fall into difficulty and become dependent on you, you shall support them; they shall live with you as though resident aliens. *Leviticus 25:35 (NRSV)*

Tuesday, November 14

I will be glad and rejoice in your love, for you saw my affliction and knew the anguish of my soul. *Psalm 31:7 (NIV)*

Wednesday, November 15

My soul melts away for sorrow; strengthen me according to your word. *Psalm 119:28 (NRSV)*

Thursday, November 16

You shall not rule over them with harshness, but shall fear your God. *Leviticus 25:43 (NRSV)*

Friday, November 17

Lift up your eyes to the sky, then look to the earth beneath; for the sky will vanish like smoke, and the earth will wear out like a garment and its inhabitants will die in like manner; but My salvation will be forever, and My righteousness will not wane. *Isaiah 51:6 (NASB)*

Saturday, November 18

Then they also will answer, "Lord, when was it that we saw you hungry or thirsty or a stranger or naked or sick or in prison, and did not take care of you?" *Matthew 25:44 (NRSV)*

Week 45: November 19-25, 2017

Who can take away suffering without entering into it?

Henri Nouwen
The Wounded Healer (72)

Sunday, November 19

The lips of the righteous feed many, but fools die for lack of sense. *Proverbs 10:21 (NRSV)*

Monday, November 20

Then I looked again at all the acts of oppression which were being done under the sun. And behold I saw the tears of the oppressed and that they had no one to comfort them; and on the side of their oppressors was power, but they had no one to comfort them. *Ecclesiastes 4:1 (NASB)*

Tuesday, November 21

When you gather the grapes of your vineyard, you shall not go over it again; it shall be for the alien, for the orphan, and for the widow. *Deuteronomy 24:21 (NASB)*

Wednesday, November 22

The wicked lie in wait for the righteous, intent on putting them to death. *Psalm 37:32 (NIV)*

Thursday, November 23 - *Thanksgiving Day*

Save us, O Lord our God, and gather us from among the nations, that we may give thanks to your holy name and glory in your praise. *Psalm 106:47 (NRSV)*

Friday, November 24

The poor will see and be glad—you who seek God, may your hearts live! *Psalm 69:32 (NIV)*

Saturday, November 25

For I know your transgressions are many and your sins are great, you who distress the righteous and accept bribes and turn aside the poor in the gate. *Amos 5:12 (NASB)*

Week 46: November 26—December 2, 2017

When people begin moving beyond charity and toward justice and solidarity with the poor and oppressed, as Jesus did, they get in trouble. Once we are actually friends with folks in struggle, we start to ask why people are poor, which is never as popular as giving to charity.

Shane Clairborne

The Irresistible Revolution (129)

Sunday, November 26

And [Samuel] said to the sons of Israel, "Thus says the Lord, the God of Israel, 'I brought Israel up from Egypt, and I delivered you from the hand of the Egyptians and from the power of all the kingdoms that were oppressing you.'" *1 Samuel 10:18 (NASB)*

Monday, November 27

Since an overseer manages God's household, [they] must be blameless—not overbearing, not quick-tempered, not given to drunkenness, not violent, not pursuing dishonest gain. *Titus 1:7 (NIV)*

Tuesday, November 28

Deliver me from the sword, my precious life from the power of the dogs. *Psalm 22:20 (NIV)*

Wednesday, November 29

I will save the lame and gather the outcast, and I will turn their shame into praise and renown in all the earth. *Zephaniah 3:19b (NASB)*

Thursday, November 30

The good [one] out of the good treasure of [their] heart brings forth what is good; and the evil [one] out of the evil treasure brings forth what is evil. *Luke 6:45a (NASB)*

Friday, December 1

Do not deliver the soul of Your turtledove to the wild beast; do not forget the life of Your afflicted forever. *Psalm 74:19 (NASB)*

Saturday, December 2

For after all it is only just for God to repay with affliction those who afflict you. *2 Thessalonians 1:6 (NASB)*

Week 47: December 3-9, 2017

Whenever we reduce the poor from people with names to abstractions, we add to their poverty and impoverish ourselves. Our point of departure for a Christian understanding of poverty is to remember that the poor are people with names, people to whom God has given gifts, and people with whom and among whom God has been working before we even arrived.

Bryant L. Myers
Walking with the Poor (106)

Sunday, December 3 - *First Sunday in Advent*

I wait for your salvation, Lord, and I follow your commands.
Psalm 119:166 (NIV)

Monday, December 4

Listen to me, you who pursue righteousness, who seek the Lord:
look to the rock from which you were hewn and to the quarry from
which you were dug. *Isaiah 51:1 (NASB)*

Tuesday, December 5

If any cannot afford the equivalent, they shall be brought before
the priest and the priest shall assess them; the priest shall assess
them according to what each one making a vow can afford.
Leviticus 27:8 (NRSV)

Wednesday, December 6

Though they plot evil against you and devise wicked schemes, they
cannot succeed. *Psalm 21:11 (NIV)*

Thursday, December 7

I love you, Lord, my strength. *Psalm 18:1 (NIV)*

Friday, December 8

With God we shall do valiantly; it is he who will tread down our
foes. *Psalm 108:13 (NRSV)*

Saturday, December 9

Better to be poor and walk in integrity than to be crooked in one's
ways even though rich. *Proverbs 28:6 (NRSV)*

Week 48: December 10-16, 2017

There is always reason to hope, even when our eyes are filled with tears.

Henri Nouwen
¡Gracias! (179)

Sunday, December 10 - *Second Sunday in Advent*

I wait for the Lord, my whole being waits, and in his word I put my hope. *Psalm 130:5 (NIV)*

Monday, December 11

Do all these evildoers know nothing? They devour my people as though eating bread; they never call on the Lord. But there they are, overwhelmed with dread, for God is present in the company of the righteous. *Psalm 14:4-5 (NIV)*

Tuesday, December 12

Lord, you are the God who saves me; day and night I cry out to you. *Psalm 88:1 (NIV)*

Wednesday, December 13

The way of the Lord is a stronghold for the upright, but destruction for evildoers. *Proverbs 10:29 (NRSV)*

Thursday, December 14

Now, brethren, we wish to make known to you the grace of God which has been given in the churches of Macedonia, that in a great ordeal of affliction their abundance of joy and their deep poverty overflowed in the wealth of their liberality. *2 Corinthians 8:1-2 (NASB)*

Friday, December 15

With long life I will satisfy [them] and show [them] my salvation. *Psalm 91:16 (NIV)*

Saturday, December 16

Blessed are those who have regard for the weak; the Lord delivers them in times of trouble. *Psalm 41:1 (NIV)*

Week 49: December 17-23, 2017

It cannot be denied that too often the weight of the Christian movement has been on the side of the strong and the powerful and against the weak and oppressed—this, despite the gospel.

Howard Thurman
Jesus and the Disinherited (20)

Sunday, December 17 - *Third Sunday in Advent*

We wait in hope for the Lord; he is our help and our shield. *Psalm 33:20 (NIV)*

Monday, December 18

I tell you, he will quickly grant justice to them. And yet, when the Son of Man comes, will he find faith on earth? *Luke 18:8 (NRSV)*

Tuesday, December 19

How long will you defend the unjust and show partiality to the wicked? *Psalm 82:2 (NIV)*

Wednesday, December 20

From heaven the Lord looked at the earth, to hear the groans of the prisoners, to set free those who were doomed to die. *Psalm 102:19b-20 (NRSV)*

Thursday, December 21

My tongue will proclaim your righteousness, your praises all day long. *Psalm 35:28 (NIV)*

Friday, December 22

Grace to you and peace from God our Father and the Lord Jesus Christ. *Philippians 1:2 (NRSV)*

Saturday, December 23

All day long the wicked covet, but the righteous give and do not hold back. *Proverbs 21:26 (NRSV)*

Week 50: December 24-30, 2017

In coming vulnerably into creation God is not giving up the characteristics of divinity, but most fully manifesting them.

William C. Placher
Narratives of a Vulnerable God (15)

Sunday, December 24 - *Christmas Eve, Fourth Sunday in Advent*

I waited patiently for the Lord; he turned to me and heard my cry. *Psalm 40:1 (NIV)*

Monday, December 25 - *Christmas Day*

"They shall name him Emmanuel," which means, "God is with us." *Matthew 1:23b (NRSV)*

Tuesday, December 26

"There is no peace for the wicked," says the Lord. *Isaiah 48:22 (NASB)*

Wednesday, December 27

The wicked earn no real gain, but those who sow righteousness get a true reward. *Proverbs 11:18 (NRSV)*

Thursday, December 28

You love righteousness and hate wickedness; therefore God, your God, has set you above your companions by anointing you with the oil of joy. *Psalm 45:7 (NIV)*

Friday, December 29

But I trust in your unfailing love; my heart rejoices in your salvation. *Psalm 13:5 (NIV)*

Saturday, December 30

May the God of hope fill you with all joy and peace as you trust in him, so that you may overflow with hope by the power of the Holy Spirit. *Romans 15:13 (NIV)*

2018

Week 51:
December 31, 2017—January 6, 2018

The mystery of the poor is this: That they are Jesus, and what you do for them you do for Him.

Dorothy Day
The Catholic Worker

Sunday, December 31

And if you give yourself to the hungry and satisfy the desire of the afflicted, then your light will rise in darkness and your gloom will become like midday. *Isaiah 58:10 (NASB)*

Monday, January 1 - *New Year's Day*

That is why we labor and strive, because we have put our hope in the living God, who is the Savior of all people, and especially of those who believe. *1 Timothy 4:10 (NIV)*

Tuesday, January 2

May Your lovingkindness also come to me, O Lord, Your salvation according to Your word. *Psalm 119:41 (NASB)*

Wednesday, January 3

Behold, the rulers of Israel, each according to his power, have been in you for the purpose of shedding blood. They have treated father and mother lightly within you. The alien they have oppressed in your midst; the fatherless and the widow they have wronged in you. *Ezekiel 22:6-7 (NASB)*

Thursday, January 4

How lovely on the mountains are the feet of him who brings good news, who announces peace and brings good news of happiness, who announces salvation, and says to Zion, "Your God reigns!" *Isaiah 52:7 (NASB)*

Friday, January 5

But you shall keep my statutes and my ordinances and commit none of these abominations, either the citizen or the alien who resides among you. *Leviticus 18:26 (NRSV)*

Saturday, January 6

Violence has grown into a rod of wickedness. None of them shall remain, none of their people, none of their wealth, nor anything eminent among them. *Ezekiel 7:11 (NASB)*

Week 52: January 7-13, 2018

The cross was God's critique of power—white power—with powerless love, snatching victory out of defeat. The sufferings of black people during slavery are too deep for words. That suffering did not end with emancipation.

James H. Cone
The Cross and the Lynching Tree (2)

Sunday, January 7

This poor man cried, and the Lord heard him and saved him out of all his troubles. *Psalm 34:6 (NASB)*

Monday, January 8

Better the poor walking in integrity than one perverse of speech who is a fool. *Proverbs 19:1 (NRSV)*

Tuesday, January 9

For you always have the poor with you, and you can show kindness to them whenever you wish; but you will not always have me. *Mark 14:7 (NRSV)*

Wednesday, January 10

Those who walk righteously and speak what is right, who reject gain from extortion and keep their hands from accepting bribes, who stop their ears against plots of murder and shut their eyes against contemplating evil—they are the ones who will dwell on the heights, whose refuge will be the mountain fortress. Their bread will be supplied, and water will not fail them. *Isaiah 33:15-16 (NIV)*

Thursday, January 11

He said, "If now I have found favor in Your sight, O Lord, I pray, let the Lord go along in our midst, even though the people are so obstinate, and pardon our iniquity and our sin, and take us as Your own possession." *Exodus 34:9 (NASB)*

Friday, January 12

For the sake of my family and friends, I will say, "Peace be within you." *Psalm 122:8 (NIV)*

Saturday, January 13

But I will encamp at my temple to guard it against marauding forces. Never again will an oppressor overrun my people, for now I am keeping watch. *Zechariah 9:8 (NIV)*

Week 53: January 14-20, 2018

The church's good name is not a matter of being on good terms
with the powerful.

Oscar A. Romero
The Violence of Love (191)

Sunday, January 14

Yes, my soul, find rest in God; my hope comes from [God].
Psalm 62:5 (NIV)

Monday, January 15 - *Martin Luther King Day*

Lord, hear my voice. Let your ears be attentive to my cry for mercy.
Psalm 130:2 (NIV)

Tuesday, January 16

Far be it from You to do such a thing, to slay the righteous with
the wicked, so that the righteous and the wicked are treated alike.
Far be it from You! Shall not the Judge of all the earth deal justly?
Genesis 18:25 (NASB)

Wednesday, January 17

Whenever the Lord raised up judges for them, the Lord was with the
judge, and [the Lord] delivered them from the hand of their enemies
all the days of the judge; for the Lord would be moved to pity by
their groaning because of those who persecuted and oppressed
them. *Judges 2:18 (NRSV)*

Thursday, January 18

For the sorrow that is according to the will of God produces a
repentance without regret, leading to salvation, but the sorrow of
the world produces death. *2 Corinthians 7:10 (NASB)*

Friday, January 19

The righteous will be glad when they are avenged, when they dip
their feet in the blood of the wicked. *Psalm 58:10 (NIV)*

Saturday, January 20

[God] has raised up a mighty savior for us in the house of [God's]
servant David. *Luke 1:69 (NRSV)*

Week 54: January 21-27, 2018

Within the very forces able to render religion a legitimator of the world are revolutionary impulses able to change the world.

Michael O. Emerson and Christian Smith
Divided by Faith (18)

Sunday, January 21

My mouth will tell of your righteous deeds, of your saving acts all day long—though I know not how to relate them all. *Psalm 71:15 (NIV)*

Monday, January 22

Even from birth the wicked go astray; from the womb they are wayward, spreading lies. *Psalm 58:3 (NIV)*

Tuesday, January 23

You gave them into the hands of their enemies, who made them suffer. Then in the time of their suffering they cried out to you and you heard them from heaven, and according to your great mercies you gave them saviors who saved them from the hands of their enemies. *Nehemiah 9:27 (NRSV)*

Wednesday, January 24

[God] will take pity on the weak and the needy and save the needy from death. *Psalm 72:13 (NIV)*

Thursday, January 25

The Lord tears down the house of the proud, but maintains the widow's boundaries. *Proverbs 15:25 (NRSV)*

Friday, January 26

I trusted in the Lord when I said, "I am greatly afflicted." *Psalm 116:10 (NIV)*

Saturday, January 27

Whoever is slow to anger has great understanding, but one who has a hasty temper exalts folly. *Proverbs 14:29 (NRSV)*

Week 55: January 28—February 3, 2018

Many men cry "Peace! Peace!" but they refuse to do the things that make for peace.

Martin Luther King, Jr.
Where Do We Go from Here:
Chaos or Community? (182)

Sunday, January 28

But now faith, hope, love, abide these three; but the greatest of these is love. *1 Corinthians 13:13 (NASB)*

Monday, January 29

The poor will eat and be satisfied; those who seek the Lord will praise [God]—may your hearts live forever! *Psalm 22:26 (NIV)*

Tuesday, January 30

The Lord lift up [the Lord's] countenance upon you, and give you peace. *Numbers 6:26 (NRSV)*

Wednesday, January 31

The afflicted also will increase their gladness in the Lord, and the needy of mankind will rejoice in the Holy One of Israel. *Isaiah 29:19 (NASB)*

Thursday, February 1

Vindicate me, Lord, for I have led a blameless life; I have trusted in the Lord and have not faltered. *Psalm 26:1 (NIV)*

Friday, February 2

My soul is bereft of peace; I have forgotten what happiness is. *Lamentations 3:17 (NRSV)*

Saturday, February 3

Therefore the Lord longs to be gracious to you, and therefore [the Lord] waits on high to have compassion on you. *Isaiah 30:18a (NASB)*

Week 56: February 4-10, 2018

Hospitality is the ability to pay attention to the guest.

Henri Nouwen
The Wounded Healer (89)

Sunday, February 4

Do not be overcome by evil, but overcome evil with good.
Romans 12:21 (NASB)

Monday, February 5

A spirit of justice for him who sits in judgment, a strength to those
who repel the onslaught at the gate. *Isaiah 28:6 (NASB)*

Tuesday, February 6

You shall not render an unjust judgment; you shall not be partial
to the poor or defer to the great: with justice you shall judge your
neighbor. *Leviticus 19:15 (NRSV)*

Wednesday, February 7

If you see the donkey of someone who hates you fallen down
under its load, do not leave it there; be sure you help them with it.
Exodus 23:5 (NIV)

Thursday, February 8

The Lord sustains the humble but casts the wicked to the ground.
Psalm 147:6 (NIV)

Friday, February 9

Thus says the Lord God, "Enough, you princes of Israel; put away
violence and destruction, and practice justice and righteousness.
Stop your expropriations from My people," declares the Lord God.
Ezekiel 45:9 (NASB)

Saturday, February 10

And the work of righteousness will be peace, and the service of
righteousness, quietness and confidence forever. *Isaiah 32:17 (NASB)*

Week 57: February 11-17, 2018

Amid the social outcast and diseased, next to the abused and dying by the roadside, between the condemned sinners, Jesus is present. Precisely where it looks most godforsaken, Jesus is intimately near.

Scott A. Bessenecker
Living Mission: The Vision and Voices of New Friars (86)

Sunday, February 11

A bruised reed He will not break and a dimly burning wick He will not extinguish; he will faithfully bring forth justice. *Isaiah 42:3 (NASB)*

Monday, February 12

Here I am; bear witness against me before the Lord and [the Lord's] anointed. Whose ox have I taken, or whose donkey have I taken, or whom have I defrauded? Whom have I oppressed, or from whose hand have I taken a bribe to blind my eyes with it? I will restore it to you. *1 Samuel 12:3 (NASB)*

Tuesday, February 13

For thus the Lord God, the Holy One of Israel, has said, "In repentance and rest you will be saved, in quietness and trust is your strength." *Isaiah 30:15a (NASB)*

Wednesday, February 14   Ash Wednesday

How long, O Lord, will I call for help, and You will not hear? I cry out to You, "Violence!" Yet You do not save. *Habakkuk 1:2 (NASB)*

Thursday, February 15

Blessed be the Lord your God who delighted in you to set you on the throne of Israel; because the Lord loved Israel forever, therefore [the Lord] made you king, to do justice and righteousness. *1 Kings 10:9 (NASB)*

Friday, February 16

These six cities shall serve as refuge for the Israelites, for the resident or transient alien among them, so that anyone who kills a person without intent may flee there. *Numbers 35:15 (NRSV)*

Saturday, February 17

Strengthen the weak hands, and make firm the feeble knees. *Isaiah 35:3 (NRSV)*

Week 58: February 18-24, 2018

Our faith in Christ, who became poor and was always close to the poor and the outcast, is the basis of our concern for the integral development of society's most neglected members.

Pope Francis
The Church of Mercy (23)

Sunday, February 18

I will appoint a place for My people Israel, and will plant them, so that they may dwell in their own place and not be moved again; and the wicked will not waste them anymore as formerly. *1 Chronicles 17:9 (NASB)*

Monday, February 19

They do not know the way of peace, and there is no justice in their tracks. *Isaiah 59:8a (NASB)*

Tuesday, February 20

They have healed the brokenness of My people superficially, saying, "Peace, peace," but there is no peace. *Jeremiah 6:14 (NASB)*

Wednesday, February 21

I will praise you with an upright heart as I learn your righteous laws. *Psalm 119:7 (NIV)*

Thursday, February 22

When we cried to the Lord, [the Lord] heard our voice, and sent an angel and brought us out of Egypt. *Numbers 20:16a (NRSV)*

Friday, February 23

When justice is done, it is a joy to the righteous, but dismay to evildoers. *Proverbs 21:15 (NRSV)*

Saturday, February 24

I rise before dawn and cry for help; I have put my hope in your word. *Psalm 119:147 (NIV)*

Week 59: February 25—March 3, 2018

The Church exists for the sake of mankind.

José Míguez Bonino
Doing Theology in a
Revolutionary Situation (68)

Sunday, February 25

The Lord is my strength and my defense; [the Lord] has become my salvation. *Psalm 118:14 (NIV)*

Monday, February 26

But when this perishable will have put on the imperishable, and this mortal will have put on immortality, then will come about the saying that is written, "Death is swallowed up in victory." *1 Corinthians 15:54 (NASB)*

Tuesday, February 27

Pride goes before destruction, and a haughty spirit before a fall. *Proverbs 16:18 (NRSV)*

Wednesday, February 28

Live in harmony with one another; do not be haughty, but associate with the lowly; do not claim to be wiser than you are. *Romans 12:16 (NRSV)*

Thursday, March 1

I was sick and you took care of me. *Matthew 25:36b (NRSV)*

Friday, March 2

Seek the Lord, all you humble of the land, you who do what he commands. Seek righteousness, seek humility; perhaps you will be sheltered on the day of the Lord's anger. *Zephaniah 2:3 (NIV)*

Saturday, March 3

My heart is in anguish within me; the terrors of death have fallen on me. *Psalm 55:4 (NIV)*

Week 60: March 4-10, 2018

I ask no favors for my sex. I surrender not our claim to equality. All I ask of our brethren is that they will take their feet from off our necks and permit us to stand upright on the ground which God has designed us to occupy.

Sarah Grimké and Angelina Grimké
On Slavery and Abolitionism:
Essays and Letters (page unavailable)

Sunday, March 4

And your righteousness will go before you; the glory of the Lord will be your rear guard. *Isaiah 58:8b (NASB)*

Monday, March 5

But you have dishonored the poor. Is it not the rich who are exploiting you? Are they not the ones who are dragging you into court? *James 2:6 (NIV)*

Tuesday, March 6

God makes a home for the lonely; [God] leads out the prisoners into prosperity, only the rebellious dwell in a parched land. *Psalm 68:6 (NASB)*

Wednesday, March 7

You always have the poor with you, but you do not always have me. *John 12:8 (NRSV)*

Thursday, March 8

Righteousness stands far away; for truth has stumbled in the street, and uprightness cannot enter. *Isaiah 59:14b (NASB)*

Friday, March 9

The salvation of the righteous comes from the Lord; [the Lord] is their stronghold in time of trouble. *Psalm 37:39 (NIV)*

Saturday, March 10

Those who have insight will shine brightly like the brightness of the expanse of heaven, and those who lead the many to righteousness, like the stars forever and ever. *Daniel 12:3 (NASB)*

Week 61: March 11-17, 2018

The Kingdom of God is a social order and not a hidden one.

John Howard Yoder
The Politics of Jesus (105)

Sunday, March 11

For the Lord will vindicate [God's] people, and will have compassion on [God's] servants, when [God] sees that their strength is gone, and there is none remaining, bond or free. *Deuteronomy 32:36 (NASB)*

Monday, March 12

With a yoke on our necks we are hard driven; we are weary, we are given no rest. *Lamentations 5:5 (NRSV)*

Tuesday, March 13

They will proclaim [the Lord's] righteousness, declaring to a people yet unborn: [the Lord] has done it! *Psalm 22:31 (NIV)*

Wednesday, March 14

I will also appoint a place for My people Israel and will plant them, that they may live in their own place and not be disturbed again, nor will the wicked afflict them any more as formerly. *2 Samuel 7:10 (NASB)*

Thursday, March 15

Yet have regard to the prayer of Your servant and to his supplication, O Lord my God, to listen to the cry and to the prayer which Your servant prays before You today. *1 Kings 8:28 (NASB)*

Friday, March 16

You are righteous, Lord, and your laws are right. *Psalm 119:137 (NIV)*

Saturday, March 17

This shall be his land for a possession in Israel; so My princes shall no longer oppress My people, but they shall give the rest of the land to the house of Israel according to their tribes. *Ezekiel 45:8 (NASB)*

Week 62: March 18-24, 2018

Privilege is a strange thing in that you notice it least when you have it most.

Debby Irving
Waking Up White,
and Finding Myself in the Story of Race (71)

Sunday, March 18

You shed abroad a plentiful rain, O God; You confirmed Your inheritance when it was parched. *Psalm 68:9 (NASB)*

Monday, March 19

This kindness is greater than that which you showed earlier: You have not run after the younger men, whether rich or poor. *Ruth 3:10b (NIV)*

Tuesday, March 20

When daylight is gone, the murderer rises up, kills the poor and needy, and in the night steals forth like a thief. *Job 24:14 (NIV)*

Wednesday, March 21

But those who want to get rich fall into temptation and a snare and many foolish and harmful desires which plunge [people] into ruin and destruction. *1 Timothy 6:9 (NASB)*

Thursday, March 22

The fear of the Lord is hatred of evil. Pride and arrogance and the way of evil and perverted speech I hate. *Proverbs 8:13 (NRSV)*

Friday, March 23

Your rulers are rebels and companions of thieves; everyone loves a bribe and chases after rewards. *Isaiah 1:23a (NASB)*

Saturday, March 24

When it goes well with the righteous, the city rejoices; and when the wicked perish, there is jubilation. *Proverbs 11:10 (NRSV)*

Week 63: March 25-31, 2018

When the crucified Jesus is called the "image of the invisible God," the meaning is that this is God, and God is like this.

Jürgen Moltmann
The Crucified God (205)

Sunday, March 25 - *Palm Sunday*

Lift up your heads, O gates! and be lifted up, O ancient doors! that the King of glory may come in. *Psalm 24:7 (NRSV)*

Monday, March 26

When the righteous are in authority, the people rejoice; but when the wicked rule, the people groan. *Proverbs 29:2 (NRSV)*

Tuesday, March 27

The mouth of the righteous utters wisdom, and [their] tongue speaks justice. *Psalm 37:30 (NASB)*

Wednesday, March 28

I have been in labor and hardship, through many sleepless nights, in hunger and thirst, often without food, in cold and exposure. *2 Corinthians 11:27 (NASB)*

Thursday, March 29

There is neither Jew nor Gentile, neither slave nor free, nor is there male and female; for you are all one in Christ Jesus. *Galatians 3:28 (NIV)*

Friday, March 30 - *Good Friday*

Surely our griefs He Himself bore, and our sorrows He carried; yet we ourselves esteemed Him stricken, smitten of God, and afflicted. *Isaiah 53:4 (NASB)*

Saturday, March 31 - *Holy Saturday*

O Hope of Israel, its Savior in time of distress, why are You like a stranger in the land or like a traveler who has pitched his tent for the night? *Jeremiah 14:8 (NASB)*

Week 64: April 1-7, 2018

But know this: God's heart for humanity is good news for the poor, comfort for the brokenhearted, and release for the captives.

Sarah Bessey
Jesus Feminist (148)

Sunday, April 1 - *Easter Sunday*

I permitted Myself to be sought by those who did not ask for Me; I permitted Myself to be found by those who did not seek Me. I said, "Here am I, here am I," to a nation which did not call on My name. *Isaiah 65:1 (NASB)*

Monday, April 2

Righteous are You, O Lord, that I would plead my case with You; indeed I would discuss matters of justice with You: Why has the way of the wicked prospered? Why are all those who deal in treachery at ease? *Jeremiah 12:1 (NASB)*

Tuesday, April 3

There is one lawgiver and judge who is able to save and to destroy. So who, then, are you to judge your neighbor? *James 4:12 (NRSV)*

Wednesday, April 4

I will glory in the Lord; let the afflicted hear and rejoice. *Psalm 34:2 (NIV)*

Thursday, April 5

And if I give all my possessions to feed the poor, and if I surrender my body to be burned, but do not have love, it profits me nothing. *1 Corinthians 13:3 (NASB)*

Friday, April 6

Righteousness and justice are the foundation of your throne; love and faithfulness go before you. *Psalm 89:14 (NIV)*

Saturday, April 7

Look at the birds of the air; they neither sow nor reap nor gather into barns, and yet your heavenly Father feeds them. Are you not of more value than they? *Matthew 6:26 (NRSV)*

Week 65: April 8-14, 2018

Serving means working beside the neediest of people, establishing with them first and foremost human relationships of closeness and bonds of solidarity.

Pope Francis
The Church of Mercy (106)

Sunday, April 8

I will sing of loyalty and of justice; to you, O Lord, I will sing. *Psalm 101:1 (NRSV)*

Monday, April 9

Will you speak what is unjust for God, and speak what is deceitful for Him? *Job 13:7 (NASB)*

Tuesday, April 10

Turn, Lord, and deliver me; save me because of your unfailing love. *Psalm 6:4 (NIV)*

Wednesday, April 11

I will make justice the measuring line and righteousness the level; then hail will sweep away the refuge of lies and the waters will overflow the secret place. *Isaiah 28:17 (NASB)*

Thursday, April 12

For you, Lord, have delivered me from death, my eyes from tears, my feet from stumbling. *Psalm 116:8 (NIV)*

Friday, April 13

The violence of the wicked will sweep them away, because they refuse to do what is just. *Proverbs 21:7 (NRSV)*

Saturday, April 14

"Cursed is he who distorts the justice due an alien, orphan, and widow." And all the people shall say, "Amen." *Deuteronomy 27:19 (NASB)*

Week 66: April 15-21, 2018

Shalom is always tested on the margins of a society and revealed by how the poor, oppressed, disempowered, and needy are treated.

Randy S. Woodley
Shalom and the Community of Creation (15)

Sunday, April 15

For the moth will eat [evil ones] like a garment, and the grub will eat them like wool. But My righteousness will be forever, and My salvation to all generations. *Isaiah 51:8 (NASB)*

Monday, April 16

The enemy will not get the better of him; the wicked will not oppress him. *Psalm 89:22 (NIV)*

Tuesday, April 17

"For I will restore you to health and I will heal you of your wounds," declares the Lord, "because they have called you an outcast, saying: 'It is Zion; no one cares for her.'" *Jeremiah 30:17 (NASB)*

Wednesday, April 18

The Lord is the strength of his people, a fortress of salvation for his anointed one. *Psalm 28:8 (NIV)*

Thursday, April 19

I was thirsty and you gave me nothing to drink. *Matthew 25:42b (NRSV)*

Friday, April 20

Grace and peace from God the Father and Christ Jesus our Savior. *Titus 1:4b (NIV)*

Saturday, April 21

Salt is good; but if salt has lost its saltiness, how can you season it? Have salt in yourselves, and be at peace with one another. *Mark 9:50 (NRSV)*

Week 67: April 22-28, 2018

Lean into the pain. Stay there in the questions, in the doubts, in the wonderings and loneliness, the tension of living in the Now and the Not Yet of the Kingdom of God.

Sarah Bessey
Jesus Feminist (52)

Sunday, April 22

Hear my prayer, Lord; listen to my cry for mercy. *Psalm 86:6 (NIV)*

Monday, April 23

You shall not follow the masses in doing evil, nor shall you testify in a dispute so as to turn aside after a multitude in order to pervert justice. *Exodus 23:2 (NASB)*

Tuesday, April 24

Let him rely on My protection, let him make peace with Me, let him make peace with Me. *Isaiah 27:5 (NASB)*

Wednesday, April 25

May mercy, peace, and love be yours in abundance. *Jude 1:2 (NRSV)*

Thursday, April 26

By justice a king gives stability to the land, but one who makes heavy exactions ruins it. *Proverbs 29:4 (NRSV)*

Friday, April 27

May the Lord reward your work, and your wages be full from the Lord, the God of Israel, under whose wings you have come to seek refuge. *Ruth 2:12 (NASB)*

Saturday, April 28

And it shall come about that when he cries out to Me, I will hear him, for I am gracious. *Exodus 22:27b (NASB)*

Week 68: April 29—May 5, 2018

As we inhabit the mind of Christ, we learn to see the world anew. Free from the stories that held us captive, we forget the categories that used to be so certain in our minds. We learn to question easy assumptions about tribe, race, ethnicity, and nation.

Emmanuel Katongole
Mirror to the Church (71)

Sunday, April 29

Better the little that the righteous have than the wealth of many wicked. *Psalm 37:16 (NIV)*

Monday, April 30

He gives his bread to the hungry and covers the naked with clothing. *Ezekiel 18:16b (NASB)*

Tuesday, May 1

Everyone who acts unjustly is an abomination to the Lord your God. *Deuteronomy 25:16b (NASB)*

Wednesday, May 2

The scorched land will become a pool and the thirsty ground springs of water; in the haunt of jackals, its resting place, grass becomes reeds and rushes. *Isaiah 35:7 (NASB)*

Thursday, May 3

The angel of the Lord encamps around those who fear him, and he delivers them. *Psalm 34:7 (NIV)*

Friday, May 4

"In that day," declares the Lord, "I will assemble the lame and gather the outcasts, even those whom I have afflicted." *Micah 4:6 (NASB)*

Saturday, May 5

How then will one answer the messengers of the nation? That the Lord has founded Zion, and the afflicted of His people will seek refuge in it. *Isaiah 14:32 (NASB)*

Week 69: May 6-12, 2018

The opposite of poverty is not wealth. In too many places, the opposite of poverty is justice.

Bryan Stevenson
Just Mercy: A Story of
Justice and Redemption (18)

Sunday, May 6

For I, the Lord, love justice, I hate robbery in the burnt offering; and I will faithfully give them their recompense and make an everlasting covenant with them. *Isaiah 61:8 (NASB)*

Monday, May 7

The mouth of the righteous is a fountain of life, but the mouth of the wicked conceals violence. *Proverbs 10:11 (NRSV)*

Tuesday, May 8

For the ruthless will come to an end and the scorner will be finished, indeed all who are intent on doing evil will be cut off. *Isaiah 29:20 (NASB)*

Wednesday, May 9

Hungry and thirsty, their soul fainted within them. Then they cried to the Lord in their trouble, and he delivered them from their distress. *Psalm 107:5 6 (NRSV)*

Thursday, May 10

For a fool speaks nonsense, and his heart inclines toward wickedness: to practice ungodliness and to speak error against the Lord, to keep the hungry person unsatisfied and to withhold drink from the thirsty. *Isaiah 32:6 (NASB)*

Friday, May 11

Indignation grips me because of the wicked, who have forsaken your law. *Psalm 119:53 (NIV)*

Saturday, May 12

You shall have honest balances, honest weights, an honest ephah, and an honest hin: I am the Lord your God, who brought you out of the land of Egypt. *Leviticus 19:36 (NRSV)*

Week 70: May 13-19, 2018

The responsibility of love is to love.

Howard Thurman
Mysticism and the Experience of Love (21)

Sunday, May 13

Blessed are the peacemakers, for they shall be called [people] of God. *Matthew 5:9 (NASB)*

Monday, May 14

Therefore I, the prisoner of the Lord, implore you to walk in a manner worthy of the calling with which you have been called, with all humility and gentleness, with patience, showing tolerance for one another in love, being diligent to preserve the unity of the Spirit in the bond of peace. *Ephesians 4:1-3 (NASB)*

Tuesday, May 15

Relieve the troubles of my heart and free me from my anguish. *Psalm 25:17 (NIV)*

Wednesday, May 16

I will strengthen you, surely I will help you, surely I will uphold you with My righteous right hand. *Isaiah 41:10b (NASB)*

Thursday, May 17

Blessed are the pure in heart, for they will see God. *Matthew 5:8 (NRSV)*

Friday, May 18

For in the day of trouble he will keep me safe in his dwelling; he will hide me in the shelter of his sacred tent and set me high upon a rock. *Psalm 27:5 (NIV)*

Saturday, May 19

I was afflicted and about to die from my youth on; I suffer Your terrors; I am overcome. *Psalm 88:15 (NASB)*

Week 71: May 20-26, 2018

The purpose of true civilization is not to focus on higher and higher technology or greater material wealth; it is to help us live more deeply and grow more fully in the humanizing work of mutual responsibility and respect.

Vincent Harding
Hope and History (99)

Sunday, May 20 - *Pentecost Sunday*

For the kingdom of God is not a matter of eating and drinking, but of righteousness, peace and joy in the Holy Spirit. *Romans 14:17 (NIV)*

Monday, May 21

Consider the blameless, observe the upright; a future awaits those who seek peace. *Psalm 37:37 (NIV)*

Tuesday, May 22

But when a righteous man turns away from his righteousness, commits iniquity and does according to all the abominations that a wicked man does, will he live? All his righteous deeds which he has done will not be remembered for his treachery which he has committed and his sin which he has committed; for them he will die. *Ezekiel 18:24 (NASB)*

Wednesday, May 23

Clouds and thick darkness surround him; righteousness and justice are the foundation of his throne. *Psalm 97:2 (NIV)*

Thursday, May 24

The wicked band together against the righteous and condemn the innocent to death. *Psalm 94:21 (NIV)*

Friday, May 25

But woe to you who are rich, for you have received your consolation. *Luke 6:24 (NRSV)*

Saturday, May 26

For the Lord will vindicate his people and have compassion on his servants. *Psalm 135:14 (NIV)*

Week 72: May 27—June 2, 2018

Shalom is an active word; we are to seek shalom, make space for shalom, pursue the path of shalom precisely because the Way of Jesus is the way of shalom, and we are the People of Shalom.

Sarah Bessey
Jesus Feminist (168)

Sunday, May 27

Deliver the one[s] who [have] been robbed from the power of [their] oppressor. *Jeremiah 22:3b (NASB)*

Monday, May 28 - *Memorial Day*

When you go to war in your land against the adversary who oppresses you, you shall sound an alarm with the trumpets, so that you may be remembered before the Lord your God and be saved from your enemies. *Numbers 10:9 (NRSV)*

Tuesday, May 29

All the nations are as nothing before [God], they are regarded by [God] as less than nothing and meaningless. *Isaiah 40:17 (NASB)*

Wednesday, May 30

For I hate divorce, says the Lord, the God of Israel, and covering one's garment with violence, says the Lord of hosts. So take heed to yourselves and do not be faithless. *Malachi 2:16 (NRSV)*

Thursday, May 31

Proclaim good tidings of [God's] salvation from day to day. *1 Chronicles 16:23b (NASB)*

Friday, June 1

May those who want to take my life be put to shame and confusion; may all who desire my ruin be turned back in disgrace. *Psalm 70:2 (NIV)*

Saturday, June 2

And can any of you by worrying add a single hour to your span of life? *Matthew 6:27 (NRSV)*

Week 73: June 3-9, 2018

Christian hope, far from taking the place of political action, invites and demands that action in the present, in favor of the oppressed, in the light and direction of the promised future. This is the language of the gospel.

José Míguez Bonino
Doing Theology in a
Revolutionary Situation (77)

Sunday, June 3

You see that a man is justified by works and not by faith alone. *James 2:24 (NASB)*

Monday, June 4

If resident aliens among you prosper, and if any of your kin fall into difficulty with one of them and sell themselves to an alien, or to a branch of the alien's family, after they have sold themselves they shall have the right of redemption; one of their brothers may redeem them. *Leviticus 25:47-48 (NRSV)*

Tuesday, June 5

Owe no one anything, except to love one another; for the one who loves another has fulfilled the law. *Romans 13:8 (NRSV)*

Wednesday, June 6

Our inheritance has been turned over to strangers, our homes to aliens. *Lamentations 5:2 (NRSV)*

Thursday, June 7

Who shows no partiality to nobles, nor regards the rich more than the poor, for they are all the work of his hands? *Job 34:19 (NRSV)*

Friday, June 8

Jesus said to him, "If you wish to be perfect, go, sell your possessions, and give the money to the poor, and you will have treasure in heaven; then come, follow me." *Matthew 19:21 (NRSV)*

Saturday, June 9

But who has stood in the council of the Lord, that he should see and hear [God's] word? Who has given heed to [God's] word and listened? *Jeremiah 23:18 (NASB)*

Week 74: June 10-16, 2018

Jesus presented himself, and was understood by the early church as God's intervention to transform effectively or destroy the social powers, practices, institutions, and ideologies that dehumanized.

Walter Brueggemann
Peace (115)

Sunday, June 10

Your throne, O God, will last for ever and ever; a scepter of justice will be the scepter of your kingdom. *Psalm 45:6 (NIV)*

Monday, June 11

His strength is famished, and calamity is ready at his side. *Job 18:12 (NASB)*

Tuesday, June 12

I am giving you these commands so that you may love one another. *John 15:17 (NRSV)*

Wednesday, June 13

And [God] saw that there was no man, and was astonished that there was no one to intercede; then [God's] own arm brought salvation to [God], and [God's] righteousness upheld [God]. *Isaiah 59:16 (NASB)*

Thursday, June 14

You shall not pervert the justice due an alien or an orphan, nor take a widow's garment in pledge. *Deuteronomy 24:17 (NASB)*

Friday, June 15

The afflicted and needy are seeking water, but there is none, and their tongue is parched with thirst; I, the Lord, will answer them Myself, as the God of Israel I will not forsake them. *Isaiah 41:17 (NASB)*

Saturday, June 16

Blessed are you who weep now, for you shall laugh. *Luke 6:21b (NASB)*

Week 75: June 17-23, 2018

Racism is not mere individual, overt prejudice or the free-floating irrational driver of race problems, but the collective misuse of power that results in diminished life opportunities for some racial groups.

Michael O. Emerson and Christian Smith
Divided by Faith (9)

Sunday, June 17

I cry out to God Most High, to God, who vindicates me.
Psalm 57:2 (NIV)

Monday, June 18

Perhaps the Lord will look on my affliction and return good to me instead of his cursing this day. *2 Samuel 16:12 (NASB)*

Tuesday, June 19

Salvation is far from the wicked, for they do not seek out your decrees. *Psalm 119:155 (NIV)*

Wednesday, June 20

[God] gives strength to the weary, and to [those] who lack might [God] increases power. *Isaiah 40:29 (NASB)*

Thursday, June 21

Jesus said to her, "Everyone who drinks of this water will be thirsty again, but those who drink of the water that I will give them will never be thirsty. The water that I will give will become in them a spring of water gushing up to eternal life." *John 4:13-14 (NRSV)*

Friday, June 22

For the Lord your God is the God of gods and the Lord of lords, the great, the mighty, and the awesome God who does not show partiality nor take a bribe. *Deuteronomy 10:17 (NASB)*

Saturday, June 23

Because of the multitude of oppressions people cry out; they call for help because of the arm of the mighty. *Job 35:9 (NRSV)*

Week 76: June 24-30, 2018

When someone makes power an absolute and an idol and turns against God's laws, against human rights, violating the people's rights, then we cannot say that such authority comes from God.

Oscar A. Romero
The Violence of Love (150)

Sunday, June 24

The salvation of the righteous comes from the Lord; he is their stronghold in time of trouble. *Psalm 37:39 (NIV)*

Monday, June 25

From the fruit of their words good persons eat good things, but the desire of the treacherous is for wrongdoing. *Proverbs 13:2 (NRSV)*

Tuesday, June 26

In my alarm I said, "I am cut off from your sight!" Yet you heard my cry for mercy when I called to you for help. *Psalm 31:22 (NIV)*

Wednesday, June 27

On those days the Jews rid themselves of their enemies, and it was a month which was turned for them from sorrow into gladness and from mourning into a holiday; that they should make them days of feasting and rejoicing and sending portions of food to one another and gifts to the poor. *Esther 9:22 (NASB)*

Thursday, June 28

May my cry come before you, Lord; give me understanding according to your word. *Psalm 119:169 (NIV)*

Friday, June 29

Woe to those who scheme iniquity, who work out evil on their beds! When morning comes, they do it, for it is in the power of their hands. They covet fields and them seize them, and houses, and take them away. *Micah 2:1-2a (NASB)*

Saturday, June 30

Righteousness guards one whose way is upright, but sin overthrows the wicked. *Proverbs 13:6 (NRSV)*

Week 77: July 1-7, 2018

We have no right to sit silently by while the inevitable seeds are sown for a harvest of disaster to our children, black and white.

W. E. B. DuBois
The Souls of Black Folk (33)

Sunday, July 1

May he judge your people in righteousness, your afflicted ones with justice. *Psalm 72:2 (NIV)*

Monday, July 2

If you address as Father the One who impartially judges according to each one's work, conduct yourselves in fear during the time of your stay on earth. *1 Peter 1:17 (NASB)*

Tuesday, July 3

[The Lord] raises up the needy out of distress. *Psalm 107:41a (NRSV)*

Wednesday, July 4 - *Independence Day*

Behold, the nations are like a drop from a bucket, and are regarded as a speck of dust on the scales; behold, [God] lifts up the islands like fine dust. *Isaiah 40:15 (NASB)*

Thursday, July 5

[The righteous one] does not lend to them at interest or take a profit from them. [The righteous] withholds [their] hand from doing wrong and judges fairly between two parties. *Ezekiel 18:8 (NIV)*

Friday, July 6

Will you even put me in the wrong? Will you condemn me that you may be justified? *Job 40:8 (NRSV)*

Saturday, July 7

My God, my rock, in whom I take refuge, my shield and the horn of my salvation, my stronghold and my refuge; my savior, You save me from violence. *2 Samuel 22:3 (NASB)*

Week 78: July 8-14, 2018

Shalom is rooted in a theology of hope, in the powerful, buoyant conviction that the world can and will be transformed and renewed, that life can and will be changed, and newness can and will come.

Walter Brueggemann
Peace (76)

Sunday, July 8

Each will be like a refuge from the wind and a shelter from the storm, like streams of water in a dry country, like the shade of a huge rock in a parched land. *Isaiah 32:2 (NASB)*

Monday, July 9

[God] will turn their own tongues against them and bring them to ruin; all who see them will shake their heads in scorn. *Psalm 64:8 (NIV)*

Tuesday, July 10

When all the prisoners of the land are crushed under foot, when human rights are perverted in the presence of the Most High, when one's case is subverted—does the Lord not see it? *Lamentations 3:34-36 (NRSV)*

Wednesday, July 11

The wicked are overthrown by their evildoing, but the righteous find a refuge in their integrity. *Proverbs 14:32 (NRSV)*

Thursday, July 12

[God] led you through the great and terrible wilderness, with its fiery serpents and scorpions and thirsty ground where there was no water; [God] brought water for you out of the rock of flint. *Deuteronomy 8:15 (NASB)*

Friday, July 13

The words of the wicked are a deadly ambush, but the speech of the upright delivers them. *Proverbs 12:6 (NRSV)*

Saturday July 14

I have certainly seen the oppression of My people in Egypt and have heard their groans, and I have come down to rescue them; come now, and I will send you to Egypt. *Acts 7:34 (NASB)*

Week 79: July 15-21, 2018

To know God is to work for justice. There is no other path to reach God.

Gustavo Gutiérrez
Gustavo Gutiérrez: Essential Writings (254)

Sunday, July 15

My salvation and my honor depend on God; he is my mighty rock, my refuge. *Psalm 62:7 (NIV)*

Monday, July 16

You shall not oppress a stranger, since you yourselves know the feelings of a stranger, for you also were strangers in the land of Egypt. *Exodus 23:9 (NASB)*

Tuesday, July 17

Blessed be the Lord your God who delighted in you, setting you on [God's] throne as king for the Lord your God; because your God loved Israel establishing them forever, therefore [God] made you king over them, to do justice and righteousness. *2 Chronicles 9:8 (NASB)*

Wednesday, July 18

Behold, to the Lord your God belong heaven and the highest heavens, the earth and all that is in it. *Deuteronomy 10:14 (NASB)*

Thursday, July 19

We were afflicted on every side: conflicts without, fears within. But God, who comforts the depressed, comforted us. *2 Corinthians 7:5b-6a (NASB)*

Friday, July 20

Whoever is faithful in a very little is faithful also in much; and whoever is dishonest in a very little is dishonest also in much. *Luke 16:10 (NRSV)*

Saturday, July 21

The righteous will inherit the land and dwell in it forever. *Psalm 37:29 (NIV)*

Week 80: July 22-28, 2018

Those who are successful in the world, those of adequate or abundant means, those in positions of power (whether they are aware of this power or not), rarely come to church to have their social and economic positions altered.

Michael O. Emerson and Christian Smith
Divided by Faith (164)

Sunday, July 22

The Lord protects and preserves [the weak]—they are counted among the blessed in the land—[God] does not give them over to the desire of their foes. *Psalm 41:2 (NIV)*

Monday, July 23

He will also strengthen you to the end, so that you may be blameless on the day of our Lord Jesus Christ. *1 Corinthians 1:8 (NRSV)*

Tuesday, July 24

[Rebellious people] must be silenced, because they are disrupting whole households by teaching things they ought not to teach—and that for the sake of dishonest gain. *Titus 1:11 (NIV)*

Wednesday, July 25

Now therefore arise, O Lord God, to Your resting place, You and the ark of Your might; let Your priests, O Lord God, be clothed with salvation and let Your godly ones rejoice in what is good. *2 Chronicles 6:41 (NASB)*

Thursday, July 26

By faith [Abraham] lived as an alien in the land of promise, as in a foreign land, dwelling in tents with Isaac and Jacob, fellow heirs of the same promise. *Hebrews 11:9 (NASB)*

Friday, July 27

But according to [God's] promise we are looking for new heavens and a new earth, in which righteousness dwells. *2 Peter 3:13 (NASB)*

Saturday, July 28

He has filled the hungry with good things, and sent the rich away empty. *Luke 1:53 (NRSV)*

Week 81: July 29—August 4, 2018

Let us live with passionate worldliness in the brilliant and fleeting time of our mortal life, and let our witness to peace grow out of the convictions of our faith, the audacity of our hope and the generosity of our love.

Charles Marsh
The Beloved Community (213)

Sunday, July 29

Blessed be the God and Father of our Lord Jesus Christ, the Father of mercies and God of all comfort, who comforts us in all our affliction so that we will be able to comfort those who are in any affliction with the comfort with which we ourselves are comforted by God. *2 Corinthians 1:3-4 (NASB)*

Monday, July 30

And he said to them, "Have you never read what David did when he and his companions were hungry and in need of food? He entered the house of God, when Abiathar was high priest, and ate the bread of the Presence, which it is not lawful for any but the priests to eat, and he gave some to his companions." *Mark 2:25-26 (NRSV)*

Tuesday, July 31

Bring water for the thirsty, O inhabitants of the land of Tema, meet the fugitive with bread. *Isaiah 21:14 (NASB)*

Wednesday, August 1

But the wisdom from above is first pure, then peaceable, gentle, reasonable, full of mercy and good fruits, unwavering, without hypocrisy. *James 3:17 (NASB)*

Thursday, August 2

I scattered them with a whirlwind among all the nations, where they were strangers. The land they left behind them was so desolate that no one traveled through it. This is how they made the pleasant land desolate. *Zechariah 7:14 (NIV)*

Friday, August 3

Be strong and take heart, all you who hope in the Lord. *Psalm 31:24 (NIV)*

Saturday, August 4

For the poor will never cease to be in the land; therefore I command you, saying, "You shall freely open your hand to your brother, to your needy and poor in your land." *Deuteronomy 15:11 (NASB)*

Week 82: August 5-11, 2018

The popularized version [of reconciliation] for white evangelicals has emphasized mainly the individual-level components, leaving the larger racialized social structures, institutions, and culture intact.

Michael O. Emerson and Christian Smith
Divided by Faith (52)

Sunday, August 5

My father made your yoke heavy, but I will add to your yoke; my father disciplined you with whips, but I will discipline you with scorpions. *1 Kings 12:14b (NASB)*

Monday, August 6

Those who were full hire themselves out for bread, but those who were hungry cease to hunger. *1 Samuel 2:5a (NASB)*

Tuesday, August 7

I said to myself, "God will judge both the righteous [one] and the wicked [one]," for a time for every matter and for every deed is there. *Ecclesiastes 3:17 (NASB)*

Wednesday, August 8

Their hands are skilled to do evil; the official and the judge ask for a bribe, and the powerful dictate what they desire; thus they pervert justice. *Micah 7:3 (NRSV)*

Thursday, August 9

Jesus had just then cured many people of diseases, plagues, and evil spirits, and had given sight to many who were blind. *Luke 7:21 (NRSV)*

Friday, August 10

The way of the wicked is an abomination to the Lord, but he loves the one who pursues righteousness. *Proverbs 15:9 (NRSV)*

Saturday, August 11

When you give alms, do not let your left hand know what your right hand is doing. *Matthew 6:3 (NRSV)*

Week 83: August 12-18, 2018

Rampant capitalism has taught the logic of profit at all costs, of giving to get, of exploitation without looking at the person . . . and we see the results in the crisis we are experiencing! This home is a place that teaches charity; it is a "school" of charity, which instructs me to go and encounter every person, not for profit, but for love.

Pope Francis
The Church of Mercy (103)

Sunday, August 12

The crooked of mind do not prosper, and the perverse of tongue fall into calamity. *Proverbs 17:20 (NRSV)*

Monday, August 13

For you have need of endurance, so that when you have done the will of God, you may receive what was promised. *Hebrews 10:36 (NASB)*

Tuesday, August 14

But let justice roll down like waters and righteousness like an ever-flowing stream. *Amos 5:24 (NASB)*

Wednesday, August 15

The Lord is righteous within her; [God] will do no injustice. Every morning [God] brings [God's] justice to light; [God] does not fail. But the unjust knows no shame. *Zephaniah 3:5 (NASB)*

Thursday, August 16

He saves the needy from the sword of their mouth, from the hand of the mighty. *Job 5:15 (NRSV)*

Friday, August 17

Whoever is pregnant with evil conceives trouble and gives birth to disillusionment. *Psalm 7:14 (NIV)*

Saturday, August 18

Hate evil, love good, and establish justice in the gate! Perhaps the Lord God of hosts may be gracious to the remnant of Joseph. *Amos 5:15 (NASB)*

Week 84: August 19-25, 2018

More preaching is not enough. What are words, however sacred and powerful, in the presence of the grim facts of the daily struggle to survive?

Howard Thurman
Jesus and the Disinherited (58)

Sunday, August 19

The heavens proclaim his righteousness, and all peoples see his glory. *Psalm 97:6 (NIV)*

Monday, August 20

The evil have no future; the lamp of the wicked will go out. *Proverbs 24:20 (NRSV)*

Tuesday, August 21

He said to me: "It is done. I am the Alpha and the Omega the Beginning and the End. To the thirsty I will give water without cost from the spring of the water of life." *Revelation 21:6 (NIV)*

Wednesday, August 22

May the foot of the proud not come against me, nor the hand of the wicked drive me away. *Psalm 36:11 (NIV)*

Thursday, August 23

He heals the brokenhearted and binds up their wounds. *Psalm 147:3 (NIV)*

Friday, August 24

I was in prison and you visited me. *Matthew 25:36c (NRSV)*

Saturday, August 25

Speak out, judge righteously, defend the rights of the poor and needy. *Proverbs 31:9 (NRSV)*

Week 85: August 26—September 1, 2018

Jesus made a feminist out of me.

Sarah Bessey
Jesus Feminist (11)

Sunday, August 26

You are God my stronghold. Why have you rejected me? Why must I go about mourning, oppressed by the enemy? *Psalm 43:2 (NIV)*

Monday, August 27

How long, Lord, will the wicked, how long will the wicked be jubilant? *Psalm 94:3 (NIV)*

Tuesday, August 28

Those who mock the poor insult their Maker; those who are glad at calamity will not go unpunished. *Proverbs 17:5 (NRSV)*

Wednesday, August 29

And again He said, "To what shall I compare the kingdom of God? It is like leaven, which a woman took and hid in three pecks of flour until it was all leavened." *Luke 13:20-21 (NASB)*

Thursday, August 30

Turn to me and be gracious to me, for I am lonely and afflicted. *Psalm 25:16 (NASB)*

Friday, August 31

But as for me, I am poor and needy; may the Lord think of me. You are my help and my deliverer; you are my God, do not delay. *Psalm 40:17 (NIV)*

Saturday, September 1

The sacrifice of the wicked is an abomination to the Lord, but the prayer of the upright is his delight. *Proverbs 15:8 (NRSV)*

Week 86: September 2-8, 2018

Christian hope is a vision and a promise for the poor, the sick, and the weak; and they hope for a new heaven and a new earth. Their hope is against the present order of injustice and slavery and for a new order of justice and peace. And unless theology takes seriously the hope of the suffering for historical liberation, it will remain irrelevant for the oppressed who view the gospel as the good news of freedom.

James H. Cone
The Spirituals and the Blues (96)

Sunday, September 2

Listen, my beloved brethren: did not God choose the poor of this world to be rich in faith and heirs of the kingdom which [God] promised to those who love [God]? *James 2:5 (NASB)*

Monday, September 3 - *Labor Day*

Commit your work to the Lord, and your plans will be established. *Proverbs 16:3 (NRSV)*

Tuesday, September 4

All flesh shall see the salvation of God. *Luke 3:6 (NRSV)*

Wednesday, September 5

I say to the Lord, "You are my God." Hear, Lord, my cry for mercy. *Psalm 140:6 (NIV)*

Thursday, September 6

A throne will even be established in lovingkindness, and a judge will sit on it in faithfulness in the tent of David; moreover, he will seek justice and be prompt in righteousness. *Isaiah 16:5 (NASB)*

Friday, September 7

A ruler who lacks understanding is a cruel oppressor; but one who hates unjust gain will enjoy a long life. *Proverbs 28:16 (NRSV)*

Saturday, September 8

You shall not pervert the justice due to your needy brother in his dispute. *Exodus 23:6 (NASB)*

Week 87: September 9-15, 2018

If sin can exist at every level of government, and in every human institution, then also the call to biblical justice in every corner of society must be sounded by those who claim a God of Justice as their Lord.

John M. Perkins
Let Justice Roll Down (185)

Sunday, September 9

The righteous know the rights of the poor; the wicked have no such understanding. *Proverbs 29:7 (NRSV)*

Monday, September 10

May those who seek my life be disgraced and put to shame; may those who plot my ruin be turned back in dismay. *Psalm 35:4 (NIV)*

Tuesday, September 11

If anyone is poor among your fellow Israelites in any of the towns of the land the Lord your God is giving you, do not be hardhearted or tightfisted toward them. *Deuteronomy 15:7 (NIV)*

Wednesday, September 12

I called to the Lord out of my distress, and [God] answered me; out of the belly of Sheol I cried, and you heard my voice. *Jonah 2:2 (NRSV)*

Thursday, September 13

Therefore, O king, may my advice be pleasing to you: break away now from your sins by doing righteousness and from your iniquities by showing mercy to the poor, in case there may be a prolonging of your prosperity. *Daniel 4:27 (NASB)*

Friday, September 14

Now in Joppa there was a disciple named Tabitha (which translated in Greek is called Dorcas); this woman was abounding with deeds of kindness and charity which she continually did. *Acts 9:36 (NASB)*

Saturday, September 15

Your statutes are always righteous; give me understanding that I may live. *Psalm 119:144 (NIV)*

Week 88: September 16-22, 2018

I dream of a church that is once again called great, even by our skeptics, because our works of mercy cannot be denied. I want no part in a movement that is deemed great because we've adopted some exceptional qualities admired by the top.

Jen Hatmaker
Interrupted (82)

Sunday, September 16

Hear my prayer, O Lord! And let my cry for help come to You. *Psalm 102:1 (NASB)*

Monday, September 17

I will betroth you to Me forever; yes, I will betroth you to Me in righteousness and in justice, in lovingkindness and in compassion. *Hosea 2:19 (NASB)*

Tuesday, September 18

Those who despise their neighbors are sinners, but happy are those who are kind to the poor. *Proverbs 14:21 (NRSV)*

Wednesday, September 19

You are my hiding place; you will protect me from trouble and surround me with songs of deliverance. *Psalm 32:7 (NIV)*

Thursday, September 20

I will clothe her priests with salvation, and her faithful people will ever sing for joy. *Psalm 132:16 (NIV)*

Friday, September 21

They shall remain with you as hired or bound laborers. They shall serve with you until the year of the jubilee. Then they and their children with them shall be free from your authority; they shall go back to their own family and return to their ancestral property. *Leviticus 25:40-41 (NRSV)*

Saturday, September 22

Though I walk in the midst of trouble, you preserve my life. You stretch out your hand against the anger of my foes; with your right hand you save me. *Psalm 138:7 (NIV)*

Week 89: September 23-29, 2018

So, go ahead and join the Eucharistic feast of God. Go to church. . . . Go to church where God is celebrated as the creator and lord of life, where the good news of God's overwhelming love permeates the congregation's understanding of itself and the world. It does not matter if the preacher is a liberal or an evangelical, a Protestant or a Catholic . . . as long as the hearts and minds are opened to the peace that passes all understanding. Go to church and let the beloved world of God slowly transform your life in compassion, mercy and grace.

Charles Marsh
The Beloved Community (215)

Sunday, September 23

Put one's mouth to the dust (there may yet be hope).
Lamentations 3:29 (NRSV)

Monday, September 24

A ruler who oppresses the poor is a beating rain that leaves no food.
Proverbs 28:3 (NRSV)

Tuesday, September 25

For [God] says, "At the acceptable time I listened to you, and on the day of salvation I helped you." Behold, now is "the acceptable time," behold, now is "the day of salvation." *2 Corinthians 6:2 (NASB)*

Wednesday, September 26

Woe to him who builds his house without righteousness and his upper rooms without justice, who uses his neighbor's services without pay and does not give him his wages. *Jeremiah 22:13 (NASB)*

Thursday, September 27

"Let the outcasts of Moab stay with you; be a hiding place to them from the destroyer." For the extortioner has come to an end, destruction has ceased, oppressors have completely disappeared from the land. *Isaiah 16:4 (NASB)*

Friday, September 28

I have taken an oath and confirmed it, that I will follow your righteous laws. *Psalm 119:106 (NIV)*

Saturday, September 29

O that my vexation were weighed, and all my calamity laid in the balances! *Job 6:2 (NRSV)*

Week 90: September 30—October 6, 2018

America owes a debt of justice which it has only begun to pay. If it loses the will to finish or slackens in its determination, history will recall its crimes and the country that would be great will lack the most indispensable element of greatness—justice.

Martin Luther King, Jr.
Where Do We Go from Here:
Chaos or Community? (109)

Sunday, September 30

O Lord, you will hear the desire of the meek; you will strengthen their heart, you will incline your ear. *Psalm 10:17 (NRSV)*

Monday, October 1

When the foundations are being destroyed, what can the righteous do? *Psalm 11:3 (NIV)*

Tuesday, October 2

Do justice for the orphan and the oppressed, so that those from earth may strike terror no more. *Psalm 10:18 (NRSV)*

Wednesday, October 3

I would have despaired unless I had believed that I would see the goodness of the Lord in the land of the living. *Psalm 27:13 (NASB)*

Thursday, October 4

Hope deferred makes the heart sick, but a desire fulfilled is a tree of life. *Proverbs 13:12 (NRSV)*

Friday, October 5

Then Jesus called his disciples to him and said, "I have compassion for the crowd, because they have been with me now for three days and have nothing to eat; and I do not want to send them away hungry, for they might faint on the way." *Matthew 15:32 (NRSV)*

Saturday, October 6

You shall not distort justice; you shall not be partial. *Deuteronomy 16:19a (NASB)*

Week 91: October 7-13, 2018

Often we think of martyrs as people who died in defense of their consciously professed faith, but Jesus' words, "What you did for the least of mine, you did for me," point to a true martyrdom in the service of God's people.

Henri Nouwen
¡Gracias! (179)

Sunday, October 7

May integrity and uprightness protect me, because my hope, Lord, is in you. *Psalm 25:21 (NIV)*

Monday, October 8

You evildoers frustrate the plans of the poor, but the Lord is their refuge. *Psalm 14:6 (NIV)*

Tuesday, October 9

The house of the wicked is destroyed, but the tent of the upright flourishes. *Proverbs 14:11 (NRSV)*

Wednesday, October 10

I give you a new commandment, that you love one another. Just as I have loved you, you also should love one another. *John 13:34 (NRSV)*

Thursday, October 11

But you shall remember that you were a slave in Egypt, and that the Lord your God redeemed you from there; therefore I am commanding you to do this thing. *Deuteronomy 24:18 (NASB)*

Friday, October 12

O our God, will you not execute judgment upon them? For we are powerless against this great multitude that is coming against us. We do not know what to do, but our eyes are on you. *2 Chronicles 20:12 (NRSV)*

Saturday, October 13

For I satisfy the weary ones and refresh everyone who languishes. *Jeremiah 31:25 (NASB)*

Week 92: October 14-20, 2018

Much of Israel's morality is concerned with the disinherited in society—widows, orphans, sojourners, all outsiders—and the clue to treating them is Israel's own experience of being an outsider [in Egypt].

Walter Brueggemann
Peace (70)

Sunday, October 14

This hope we have as an anchor of the soul, a hope both sure and steadfast and one which enters within the veil. *Hebrews 6:19 (NASB)*

Monday, October 15

Whoever plans to do evil will be called a mischief-maker. *Proverbs 24:8 (NRSV)*

Tuesday, October 16

As for me, I will always have hope; I will praise you more and more. *Psalm 71:14 (NIV)*

Wednesday, October 17

The rich is wise in self-esteem, but an intelligent poor person sees through the pose. *Proverbs 28:11 (NRSV)*

Thursday, October 18

Now may the God of peace . . . sanctify you entirely; and may your spirit and soul and body be preserved complete, without blame at the coming of our Lord Jesus Christ. *1 Thessalonians 5:23 (NASB)*

Friday, October 19

For the wicked boast of the desires of their heart, those greedy for gain curse and renounce the Lord. *Psalm 10:3 (NRSV)*

Saturday, October 20

The violent entice their neighbors, and lead them in a way that is not good. *Proverbs 16:29 (NRSV)*

Week 93: October 21-27, 2018

The Beatitudes are in fact more a revelation about God than about the poor. They tell us who God is and which kingdom is God's. They speak to us of God as the defender of the poor, as their protector, their liberator. Only in this way is it possible to grasp the privileged role of the poor—concrete poor people, the dispossessed, and the oppressed—in God's kingdom.

Gustavo Gutiérrez
Gustavo Gutiérrez: Essential Writings (105)

Sunday, October 21

So then, while we have opportunity, let us do good to all people, and especially to those who are of the household of the faith. *Galatians 6:10 (NASB)*

Monday, October 22

Morning by morning I will destroy all the wicked in the land, cutting off all evildoers from the city of the Lord. *Psalm 101:8 (NRSV)*

Tuesday, October 23

I was hungry and you gave me food. *Matthew 25:35a (NRSV)*

Wednesday, October 24

But now it has come to you, and you are impatient; it touches you, and you are dismayed. *Job 4:5 (NRSV)*

Thursday, October 25

But for you who revere my name the sun of righteousness shall rise, with healing in its wings. You shall go out leaping like calves from the stall. *Malachi 4:2 (NRSV)*

Friday, October 26

The people curse those who hold back grain, but a blessing is on the head of those who sell it. *Proverbs 11:26 (NRSV)*

Saturday, October 27

So Saul's servants spoke these words to David. But David said, "Is it trivial in your sight to become the king's son-in-law, since I am a poor man and lightly esteemed?" *1 Samuel 18:23 (NASB)*

Week 94: October 28—November 3, 2018

A community that faithfully attends to the narratives of the crucified Jesus cannot be a community that excludes.

William C. Placher
Narratives of a Vulnerable God (154)

Sunday, October 28

You must not move your neighbor's boundary marker, set up by former generations. *Deuteronomy 19:14a (NRSV)*

Monday, October, 29

I know that the Lord secures justice for the poor and upholds the cause of the needy. *Psalm 140:12 (NIV)*

Tuesday, October 30

Keep on loving one another as brothers and sisters.
Hebrews 13:1 (NIV)

Wednesday, October 31

Thus says the Lord, "Preserve justice and do righteousness, for My salvation is about to come and My righteousness to be revealed."
Isaiah 56:1 (NASB)

Thursday, November 1

A father of the fatherless and a judge for the widows, is God in His holy habitation. *Psalm 68:5 (NASB)*

Friday, November 2

Blessed is the king who comes in the name of the Lord! Peace in heaven, and glory in the highest heaven!
Luke 19:38 (NRSV)

Saturday, November 3

You shall not oppress a hired servant who is poor and needy, whether [they are] one of your countrymen or one of your aliens who is in your land in your towns. *Deuteronomy 24:14 (NASB)*

Week 95: November 4-10, 2018

Black people did not need to go to seminary and study theology to know that white Christianity was fraudulent. As a teenager in the South where whites treated blacks with contempt, I and other blacks knew that the Christian identity of whites was not a true expression of what it meant to follow Jesus.

James H. Cone
The Cross and the Lynching Tree (131)

Sunday, November 4

He fulfills the desires of those who fear him; he hears their cry and saves them. *Psalm 145:19 (NIV)*

Monday, November 5

What is desirable in a person is loyalty, and it is better to be poor than a liar. *Proverbs 19:22 (NRSV)*

Tuesday, November 6 - *Election Day*

Furthermore, you shall select out of all the people [those] who fear God, [people] of truth, those who hate dishonest gain. *Exodus 18:21a (NASB)*

Wednesday, November 7

The evil do not understand justice, but those who seek the Lord understand it completely. *Proverbs 28:5 (NRSV)*

Thursday, November 8

In the morning, when [Jesus] returned to the city, he was hungry. *Matthew 21:18 (NRSV)*

Friday, November 9

After that you will be called the city of righteousness, a faithful city. *Isaiah 1:26b (NASB)*

Saturday, November 10

I call heaven and earth to witness against you today, that I have set before you life and death, the blessing and the curse. So choose life in order that you may live, you and your descendants. *Deuteronomy 30:19 (NASB)*

Week 96: November 11-17, 2018

Let us not tire of preaching love, it is the force that will overcome the world. Let us not tire of preaching love. Though we see that waves of violence succeed in drowning the fire of Christian love, love must win out; it is the only thing that can.

Oscar A. Romero
The Violence of Love (7)

Sunday, November 11

"Which of these three do you think proved to be a neighbor to the man who fell into the robbers' hands?" And he said, "The one who showed mercy toward him." Then Jesus said to him, "Go and do the same." *Luke 10:36-37 (NASB)*

Monday, November 12

Justice, and only justice, you shall pursue, that you may live and possess the land which the Lord your God is giving you. *Deuteronomy 16:20 (NASB)*

Tuesday, November 13

We waited for peace, but no good came; for a time of healing, but behold, terror! *Jeremiah 8:15 (NASB)*

Wednesday, November 14

They will pass through the land hard-pressed and famished, and it will turn out that when they are hungry, they will be enraged and curse their king and their God as they face upward. *Isaiah 8:21 (NASB)*

Thursday, November 15

You shall not lend [the poor] your money at interest taken in advance, or provide them food at a profit. *Leviticus 25:37 (NRSV)*

Friday, November 16

All your words are true; all your righteous laws are eternal. *Psalm 119:160 (NIV)*

Saturday, November 17

"Should evil come upon us, the sword, or judgment, or pestilence, or famine, we will stand before this house and before You (for Your name is in this house) and cry to You in our distress, and You will hear and deliver us." *2 Chronicles 20:9 (NASB)*

Week 97: November 18-24, 2018

I learned more about God from the tears of homeless mothers than any systematic theology ever taught me.

Shane Claiborne
Irresistible Revolution (51)

Sunday, November 18

I will be fully satisfied as with the richest of foods; with singing lips my mouth will praise you. *Psalm 63:5 (NIV)*

Monday, November 19

The lips of the righteous know what is acceptable, but the mouth of the wicked what is perverse. *Proverbs 10:32 (NRSV)*

Tuesday, November 20

Because you have looted many nations, all the remainder of the peoples will loot you—because of human bloodshed and violence done to the land, to the town and all its inhabitants. *Habakkuk 2:8 (NASB)*

Wednesday, November 21

You have loved righteousness and hated lawlessness; therefore God, Your God, has anointed You with the oil of gladness above Your companions. *Hebrews 1:9 (NASB)*

Thursday, November 22 - *Thanksgiving Day*

"Give thanks to the Lord of hosts, for the Lord is good, for his steadfast love endures forever!" For I will restore the fortunes of the land as at first, says the Lord. *Jeremiah 33:11b (NRSV)*

Friday, November 23

I will be fully satisfied as with the richest of foods; with singing lips my mouth will praise you. *Psalm 63:5 (NIV)*

Saturday, November 24

On the last day of the festival, the great day, while Jesus was standing there, he cried out, "Let anyone who is thirsty come to me." *John 7:37 (NRSV)*

Week 98: November 25—December 1, 2018

To revile because one has been reviled—this is the real evil because it is the evil of the soul itself.

Howard Thurman
Jesus and the Disinherited (11)

Sunday, November 25

Reprove the ruthless. *Isaiah 1:17b (NASB)*

Monday, November 26

Is not your wickedness great, and your iniquities without end? *Job 22:5 (NASB)*

Tuesday, November 27

For [the evil person] never thought of doing a kindness, but hounded to death the poor and the needy and the brokenhearted. *Psalm 109:16 (NIV)*

Wednesday, November 28

The Lord God has given Me the tongue of disciples, that I may know how to sustain the weary one with a word. He awakens Me morning by morning, He awakens My ear to listen as a disciple. *Isaiah 50:4 (NASB)*

Thursday, November 29

And the congregation of those who believed were of one heart and soul; and not one of them claimed that anything belonging to [them] was [their] own, but all things were common property to them. *Acts 4:32 (NASB)*

Friday, November 30

Do not offer any part of yourself to sin as an instrument of wickedness, but rather offer yourselves to God as those who have been brought from death to life; and offer every part of yourself to him as an instrument of righteousness. *Romans 6:13 (NIV)*

Saturday, December 1

Rejoice in the Lord and be glad, you righteous; sing, all you who are upright in heart! *Psalm 32:11 (NIV)*

Week 99: December 2-8, 2018

I want a church that is poor, and for the poor.

Pope Francis
The Church of Mercy (24)

Sunday, December 2 - *First Sunday in Advent*

But if we hope for what we do not yet have, we wait for it patiently. *Romans 8:25 (NIV)*

Monday, December 3

God is a righteous judge, a God who displays his wrath every day. *Psalm 7:11 (NIV)*

Tuesday, December 4

Blessed are the meek, for they will inherit the earth. *Matthew 5:5 (NRSV)*

Wednesday, December 5

Jesus said to them again, "Peace be with you. As the Father has sent me, so I send you." *John 20:21 (NRSV)*

Thursday, December 6

Do not hide your face from your servant; answer me quickly, for I am in trouble. *Psalm 69:17 (NIV)*

Friday, December 7

So the poor have hope, and injustice shuts its mouth. *Job 5:16 (NRSV)*

Saturday, December 8

Many are the woes of the wicked, but the Lord's unfailing love surrounds the one who trusts in him. *Psalm 32:10 (NIV)*

Week 100: December 9-15, 2018

The power of just mercy is that it belongs to the undeserving. It's when mercy is least expected that it's most potent—strong enough to break the cycle of victimization and victimhood, retribution and suffering. It has the power to heal the psychic harm and injuries that lead to aggression and violence, abuse of power, mass incarceration.

Bryan Stevenson
*Just Mercy: A Story of
Justice and Redemption* (294)

Sunday, December 9 - *Second Sunday in Advent*

The Lord is good to those who wait for him, to the soul that seeks him. *Lamentations 3:25 (NRSV)*

Monday, December 10

How the faithful city has become a harlot, she who was full of justice! Righteousness once lodged in her, but now murderers. *Isaiah 1:21 (NASB)*

Tuesday, December 11

Grace to you and peace from God our Father and the Lord Jesus Christ. *Galatians 1:3 (NASB)*

Wednesday, December 12

But with righteousness He will judge the poor, and decide with fairness for the afflicted of the earth. *Isaiah 11:4a (NASB)*

Thursday, December 13

But of the Son He says, "Your throne, O God, is forever and ever, and the righteous scepter is the scepter of His kingdom." *Hebrews 1:8 (NASB)*

Friday, December 14

For where your treasure is, there your heart will be also. *Matthew 6:21 (NRSV)*

Saturday, December 15

You have delivered me from all my troubles, and my eyes have looked in triumph on my foes. *Psalm 54:7 (NIV)*

Week 101: December 16-22, 2018

These narratives of a vulnerable God are not safe stories.

William C. Placher
Narratives of a Vulnerable God (141)

Sunday, December 16 - *Third Sunday in Advent*

But as for me, I will look to the Lord, I will wait for the God of my salvation; my God will hear me. *Micah 7:7 (NRSV)*

Monday, December 17

Honest balances and scales are the Lord's; all the weights in the bag are his work. *Proverbs 16:11 (NRSV)*

Tuesday, December 18

You shall not take a bribe, for a bribe blinds the clear-sighted and subverts the cause of the just. *Exodus 23:8 (NASB)*

Wednesday, December 19

For you know the grace of our Lord Jesus Christ, that though He was rich, yet for your sake He became poor, so that you through His poverty might become rich. *2 Corinthians 8:9 (NASB)*

Thursday, December 20

When you beat your olive tree, you shall not go over the boughs again; it shall be for the alien, for the orphan, and for the widow. *Deuteronomy 24:20 (NASB)*

Friday, December 21

The lame I will make the remnant, and those who were cast off, a strong nation. *Micah 4:7a (NRSV)*

Saturday, December 22

The wicked plot against the righteous and gnash their teeth at them. *Psalm 37:12 (NIV)*

Week 102: December 23-29, 2018

God for us is who God is as God.

Catherine Mowry LaCugna
God for Us (305)

Sunday, December 23 - *Fourth Sunday in Advent*

For Your salvation I wait, O Lord. *Genesis 49:18 (NASB)*

Monday, December 24 - *Christmas Eve*

And it will be said in that day, "Behold, this is our God for whom we have waited that [God] might save us. This is the Lord for whom we have waited; let us rejoice and be glad in [God's] salvation." *Isaiah 25:9 (NASB)*

Tuesday, December 25 - *Christmas Day*

I will dwell among them. *Exodus 25:8b (NIV)*

Wednesday, December 26

The way of the guilty is crooked, but the conduct of the pure is right. *Proverbs 21:8 (NRSV)*

Thursday, December 27

Whoever says to the wicked, "You are innocent," will be cursed by peoples, abhorred by nations. *Proverbs 24:24 (NRSV)*

Friday, December 28

He will make your righteous reward shine like the dawn, your vindication like the noonday sun. *Psalm 37:6 (NIV)*

Saturday, December 29

To be a partner of a thief is to hate one's own life; one hears the victim's curse, but discloses nothing. *Proverbs 29:24 (NRSV)*

2019

Week 103:
December 30, 2018—January 5, 2019

In contrast to every other kingdom that has been and ever will be, this kingdom belongs to the poor, Jesus said, and to the peacemakers, the merciful, and those who hunger and thirst for God. In this kingdom, the people from the margins and the bottom rungs will be lifted up to places of honor, seated at the best spots at the table. This kingdom knows no geographic boundaries, no political parties, no single language or culture.

Rachel Held Evans
Searching for Sunday (252-253)

Sunday, December 30

Do not despise an Edomite, for the Edomites are related to you. Do not despise an Egyptian, because you resided as foreigners in their country. *Deuteronomy 23:7 (NIV)*

Monday, December 31

And the Egyptians treated us harshly and afflicted us, and imposed hard labor on us. *Deuteronomy 26:6 (NASB)*

Tuesday, January 1 - *New Year's Day*

You are my hiding place and my shield; I wait for Your word. *Psalm 119:114 (NASB)*

Wednesday, January 2

The highway of the upright avoids evil; those who guard their way preserve their lives. *Proverbs 16:17 (NRSV)*

Thursday, January 3

Jesus said to them, "I am the bread of life. Whoever comes to me will never be hungry, and whoever believes in me will never be thirsty." *John 6:35 (NRSV)*

Friday, January 4

Sing to the Lord, praise his name; proclaim his salvation day after day. *Psalm 96:2 (NIV)*

Saturday, January 5

To do righteousness and justice is more acceptable to the Lord than sacrifice. *Proverbs 21:3 (NRSV)*

Week 104: January 6-12, 2019

You're in the seventh inning, and one team is up twenty to nothing. Then we find out that the winning team has been cheating all along. And then they say, "Okay, okay, okay, we're sorry. Let's go back out and finish the game." Obviously, they're already twenty runs up, so that's one reason why I'm uncomfortable with kind of "Let's just go to a relationship but not really address the [structural] issues" approach.

Michael O. Emerson and Christian Smith
Divided by Faith (127)

Sunday, January 6

Blessed are the merciful, for they will receive mercy.
Matthew 5:7 (NRSV)

Monday, January 7

[The Lord] brought them out of darkness and gloom, and broke
their bonds asunder. *Psalm 107:14 (NRSV)*

Tuesday, January 8

And why do you worry about clothing? Consider the lilies of
the field, how they grow; they neither toil nor spin, yet I tell you,
even Solomon in all his glory was not clothed like one of these.
Matthew 6:28-29 (NRSV)

Wednesday, January 9

Do not bring us to the time of trial, but rescue us from the evil one.
Matthew 6:13 (NRSV)

Thursday, January 10

For the Lord is righteous, he loves justice. *Psalm 11:7a (NIV)*

Friday, January 11

The upright will see [the Lord's] face. *Psalm 11:7b (NIV)*

Saturday, January 12

Then the king said to the wise men who understood the times—for
it was the custom of the king so to speak before all who knew law
and justice. *Esther 1:13 (NASB)*

Week 105: January 13-19, 2019

Where justice is denied, where poverty is enforced, where ignorance prevails, and where any one class is made to feel that society is an organized conspiracy to oppress, rob, and degrade them, neither persons nor property will be safe.

Frederick Douglass
Frederick Douglass: Selected Speeches and Writings (699)

Sunday, January 13

Save us and help us with your right hand, that those you love may be delivered. *Psalm 60:5 (NIV)*

Monday, January 14

Why, O Lord, do you stand far off? *Psalm 10:1a (NRSV)*

Tuesday, January 15

Why do you hide yourself in times of trouble? *Psalm 10:1b (NRSV)*

Wednesday, January 16

May the God of steadfastness and encouragement grant you to live in harmony with one another, in accordance with Christ Jesus. *Romans 15:5 (NRSV)*

Thursday, January 17

After you have suffered for a little while, the God of all grace, who called you to His eternal glory in Christ, will Himself perfect, confirm, strengthen and establish you. *1 Peter 5:10 (NASB)*

Friday, January 18

Uphold me, and I will be delivered; I will always have regard for your decrees. *Psalm 119:117 (NIV)*

Saturday, January 19

Say to the righteous that it will go well with them, for they will eat the fruit of their actions. *Isaiah 3:10 (NASB)*

Week 106: January 20-26, 2019

Peace without justice is equivalent to institutionalizing injustice.

Omar Barghouti
Boycott, Divestment, Sanctions:
The Global Struggle for Palestinian Rights (83)

Sunday, January 20

Therefore justice is far from us, and righteousness does not overtake us. *Isaiah 59:9a (NASB)*

Monday, January 21 - *Martin Luther King Day*

Those who are kind reward themselves, but the cruel do themselves harm. *Proverbs 11:17 (NRSV)*

Tuesday, January 22

But the eyes of the Lord are on those who fear him, on those whose hope is in his unfailing love. *Psalm 33:18 (NIV)*

Wednesday, January 23

For all of us have become like one who is unclean, and all our righteous deeds are like a filthy garment; and all of us wither like a leaf, and our iniquities, like the wind, take us away. *Isaiah 64:6 (NASB)*

Thursday, January 24

I am overwhelmed with troubles and my life draws near to death. *Psalm 88:3 (NIV)*

Friday, January 25

All deeds are right in the sight of the doer, but the Lord weighs the heart. *Proverbs 21:2 (NRSV)*

Saturday, January 26

In my distress I called to the Lord; I cried to my God for help. From his temple he heard my voice; my cry came before him, into his ears. *Psalm 18:6 (NIV)*

Week 107: January 27—February 2, 2019

The righteousness of God is the power of God to achieve victory for the oppressed.

James H. Cone
The Spirituals and the Blues (92)

Sunday, January 27

Let all creation rejoice before the Lord, for he comes, he comes to judge the earth. *Psalm 96:13a (NIV)*

Monday, January 28

He will judge the world in righteousness and the peoples in his faithfulness. *Psalm 96:13b (NIV)*

Tuesday, January 29

Beware! Do not turn to iniquity; because of that you have been tried by affliction. *Job 36:21 (NRSV)*

Wednesday, January 30

The Spirit of the Lord God is upon me, because the Lord has anointed me to bring good news to the afflicted. *Isaiah 61:1a (NASB)*

Thursday, January 31

No harm happens to the righteous, but the wicked are filled with trouble. *Proverbs 12:21 (NRSV)*

Friday, February, 1

Did I not weep for those whose day was hard? *Job 30:25a (NRSV)*

Saturday, February 2

Was not my soul grieved for the poor? *Job 30:25b (NRSV)*

Week 108: February 3-9, 2019

In situations of inequality or oppression, the oppressed group must take a stand somewhere, sometime. For until the people take that stand, there is no development possible for them. Yet when they take that stand in the face of clear injustice, an oppressed people are once again humanized.

John M. Perkins
Let Justice Roll Down (115)

Sunday, February 3

The name of the Lord is a strong tower; the righteous run into it and are safe. *Proverbs 18:10 (NRSV)*

Monday, February 4

Then the owner of the house became angry and said to his slave, "Go out at once into the streets and lanes of the town and bring in the poor, the crippled, the blind, and the lame." *Luke 14:21b (NRSV)*

Tuesday, February 5

Both we and our ancestors have sinned; we have committed iniquity, have done wickedly. *Psalm 106:6 (NRSV)*

Wednesday, February 6

Set me free from my prison, that I may praise your name. Then the righteous will gather about me because of your goodness to me. *Psalm 142:7 (NIV)*

Thursday, February 7

There is no other God besides Me, a righteous God and a Savior. *Isaiah 45:21b (NASB)*

Friday, February 8

It is definitely because they have misled My people by saying, "Peace!" when there is no peace. And when anyone builds a wall, behold, they plaster it over with whitewash. *Ezekiel 13:10 (NASB)*

Saturday, February 9

When the wicked die, their hope perishes, and the expectation of the godless comes to nothing. *Proverbs 11:7 (NRSV)*

Week 109: February 10-16, 2019

All prejudice is evil, but the prejudice that rejects a man because of the color of his skin is the most despicable expression of a man's inhumanity to man.

Martin Luther King, Jr.
Where Do We Go from Here:
Chaos or Community? (110)

Sunday, February 10

And behold, some are last who will be first and some are first who will be last. *Luke 13:30 (NASB)*

Monday, February 11

The Righteous One observes the house of the wicked; he casts the wicked down to ruin. *Proverbs 21:12 (NRSV)*

Tuesday, February 12

[The wicked king] oppresses the poor and needy, commits robbery, does not restore a pledge, but lifts up his eyes to the idols and commits abomination. *Ezekiel 18:12 (NASB)*

Wednesday, February 13

[God] said to them, "Here is rest, give rest to the weary," and, "Here is repose," but they would not listen. *Isaiah 28:12 (NASB)*

Thursday, February 14

But Nebuzaradan the captain of the guard left some of the poorest of the land to be vinedressers and plowmen. *Jeremiah 52:16 (NASB)*

Friday, February 15

[The beast] will speak out against the Most High and wear down the saints of the Highest One, and he will intend to make alterations in times and in law; and they will be given into his hand for a time. *Daniel 7:25 (NASB)*

Saturday, February 16

[The good king] keeps his hand from the poor, does not take interest or increase, but executes My ordinances, and walks in My statutes; he will not die for his father's iniquity, he will surely live. *Ezekiel 18:17 (NASB)*

Week 110: February 17-23, 2019

Once we have seen the suffering Christ within us, we will see him wherever we see people in pain.

Henri Nouwen
¡Gracias! (31)

Sunday, February 17

You have rejected us, God, and burst upon us; you have been angry—now restore us! *Psalm 60:1 (NIV)*

Monday, February 18

[The good person does not] oppress anyone, or retain a pledge, or commit robbery. *Ezekiel 18:16a (NASB)*

Tuesday, February 19

Come, buy wine and milk without money and without cost. *Isaiah 55:1b (NASB)*

Wednesday, February 20

Rescue the weak and the needy; deliver them from the hand of the wicked. *Psalm 82:4 (NIV)*

Thursday, February 21

Your eyes are too pure to approve evil, and You can not look on wickedness with favor. Why do You look with favor on those who deal treacherously? Why are You silent when the wicked swallow up those more righteous than they? *Habakkuk 1:13 (NASB)*

Friday, February 22

In this manner Absalom dealt with all Israel who came to the king for judgment; so Absalom stole away the hearts of the men of Israel. *2 Samuel 15:6 (NASB)*

Saturday, February 23

They cause the poor to go about naked without clothing. *Job 24:10a (NASB)*

Week 111: February 24—March 2, 2019

We need you: your voice rising, your hands working. You matter in this story.

Sarah Bessey
Jesus Feminist (183)

Sunday, February 24

If any woman who is a believer has dependent widows, she must assist them and the church must not be burdened, so that it may assist those who are widows indeed. *1 Timothy 5:16 (NASB)*

Monday, February 25

You shall not have in your bag two kinds of weights, large and small. *Deuteronomy 25:13 (NRSV)*

Tuesday, February 26

The mind of the righteous ponders how to answer. *Proverbs 15:28a (NRSV)*

Wednesday, February 27

The mouth of the wicked pours out evil. *Proverbs 15:28b (NRSV)*

Thursday, February 28

For each tree is known by its own fruit. For [people] do not gather figs from thorns, nor do they pick grapes from a briar bush. *Luke 6:44 (NASB)*

Friday, March 1

They cried to the Lord in their trouble, and he saved them from their distress. *Psalm 107:19 (NRSV)*

Saturday, March 2

"Do not be afraid of the king of Babylon, whom you are now fearing; do not be afraid of him," declares the Lord, "for I am with you to save you and deliver you from his hand." *Jeremiah 42:11 (NASB)*

Week 112: March 3-9, 2019

The Bible is not romantic about its vision. It never assumes *shalom* will come naturally or automatically. *Shalom* in a special way is the task and burden of the well-off and powerful. They are the ones held accountable for *shalom*.

Walter Brueggemann
Peace (19)

Sunday, March 3

From daughter Zion has departed all her majesty. Her princes have become like stags that find no pasture; they fled without strength before the pursuer. *Lamentations 1:6 (NRSV)*

Monday, March 4

But your eyes and your heart are intent only upon your own dishonest gain, and on shedding innocent blood and on practicing oppression and extortion. *Jeremiah 22:17 (NASB)*

Tuesday, March 5

May all who want to take my life be put to shame and confusion. *Psalm 40:14a (NIV)*

Wednesday, March 6 - *Ash Wednesday*

Out of the depths I cry to you, Lord. *Psalm 130:1 (NIV)*

Thursday, March 7

May all who desire my ruin be turned back in disgrace. *Psalm 40:14b (NIV)*

Friday, March 8

Let us not lose heart in doing good, for in due time we will reap if we do not grow weary. *Galatians 6:9 (NASB)*

Saturday, March 9

If the righteous are repaid on earth, how much more the wicked and the sinner! *Proverbs 11:31 (NRSV)*

Week 113: March 10-16, 2019

Caring about truth in every dimension of the Church's life and of Christians' lives is a necessary foundation for . . . justice building, peacemaking, hospitality, and gospel proclaiming.

Marva J. Dawn
Powers, Weakness, and
the Tabernacling of God (138)

Sunday, March 10

Therefore, thus says the Lord, "If you return, then I will restore you." *Jeremiah 15:19a (NASB)*

Monday, March 11

He has fixed a day in which He will judge the world in righteousness. *Acts 17:31a (NASB)*

Tuesday, March 12

He does not keep the wicked alive, but gives justice to the afflicted. *Job 36:6 (NASB)*

Wednesday, March 13

For the grace of God has appeared that offers salvation to all people. *Titus 2:11 (NIV)*

Thursday, March 14

I lead a blameless life; deliver me and be merciful to me. *Psalm 26:11 (NIV)*

Friday, March 15

And our hope for you is firmly grounded, knowing that as you are sharers of our sufferings, so also you are sharers of our comfort. *2 Corinthians 1:7 (NASB)*

Saturday, March 16

I cry to you, Lord; I say, "You are my refuge, my portion in the land of the living." *Psalm 142:5 (NIV)*

Week 114: March 17-23, 2019

The word *solidarity* is a little worn and at times poorly understood, but it refers to something more than a few sporadic acts of generosity. It presumes the creation of a new mind-set that thinks in terms of community and the priority of the life of all over the appropriation of goods by a few.

Pope Francis
The Church of Mercy (24)

Sunday, March 17

They plot injustice and say, "We have devised a perfect plan!" Surely the human mind and heart are cunning. *Psalm 64:6 (NIV)*

Monday, March 18

Now a traveler came to the rich man, and he was unwilling to take from his own flock or his own herd, to prepare for the wayfarer who had come to him; rather he took the poor man's ewe lamb and prepared it for the man who had come to him. *2 Samuel 12:4 (NASB)*

Tuesday, March 19

But there was found in it a poor wise man and he delivered the city by his wisdom. Yet no one remembered that poor man. *Ecclesiastes 9:15 (NASB)*

Wednesday, March 20

They will throw dust on their heads, and with weeping and mourning cry out: "Woe! Woe to you, great city, where all who had ships on the sea became rich through her wealth! In one hour she has been brought to ruin!" *Revelation 18:19 (NIV)*

Thursday, March 21

Can I tolerate wicked scales and a bag of dishonest weights? *Micah 6:11 (NRSV)*

Friday, March 22

[God] will swallow up death for all time, and the Lord God will wipe tears away from all faces, and [God] will remove the reproach of [God's] people from all the earth; for the Lord has spoken. *Isaiah 25:8 (NASB)*

Saturday, March 23

For [God] stands at the right hand of the needy to save their lives from those who would condemn them. *Psalm 109:31 (NIV)*

Week 115: March 24-30, 2019

God . . . is clearly and unequivocally on the side of the poor.

José Míguez Bonino
Doing Theology in a
Revolutionary Situation (112)

Sunday, March 24

Have You completely rejected Judah? Or have You loathed Zion?
Why have You stricken us so that we are beyond healing? We waited
for peace, but nothing good came; and for a time of healing, but
behold, terror! *Jeremiah 14:19 (NASB)*

Monday, March 25

"O death, where is your victory? O death, where is your sting?"
1 Corinthians 15:55 (NASB)

Tuesday, March 26

May your unfailing love be with us, Lord, even as we put our hope in
you. *Psalm 33:22 (NIV)*

Wednesday, March 27

But you do see! Indeed you note trouble and grief, that you may take
it into your hands. *Psalm 10:14a (NRSV)*

Thursday, March 28

The helpless commit themselves to you. *Psalm 10:14b (NRSV)*

Friday, March 29

You have been the helper of the orphan. *Psalm 10:14c (NRSV)*

Saturday, March 30

One who walks in integrity will be safe, but whoever follows
crooked ways will fall into the Pit. *Proverbs 28:18 (NRSV)*

Week 116: March 31—April 6, 2019

The daughters of the earth are crying out for God's justice and peace. First and third world and caught somewhere in between, we are buried in the world's power structures, tensions, histories, the old empire fallout of authority and patriarchy, war and economic injustice, hierarchy and systemic evils generation after generation.

Sarah Bessey
Jesus Feminist (159)

Sunday, March 31

A good name is to be chosen rather than great riches, and favor is better than silver or gold. *Proverbs 22:1 (NRSV)*

Monday, April 1

But a Samaritan, who was on a journey, came upon him; and when he saw him, he felt compassion, and came to him and bandaged up his wounds, pouring oil and wine on them; and he put him on his own beast, and brought him to an inn and took care of him. *Luke 10:33-34 (NASB)*

Tuesday, April 2

[The foreigners] shall live with you in your midst, in the place which [they] shall choose in one of your towns where it pleases [them]; you shall not mistreat [them]. *Deuteronomy 23:16 (NASB)*

Wednesday, April 3

The wicked covet the proceeds of wickedness, but the root of the righteous bears fruit. *Proverbs 12:12 (NRSV)*

Thursday, April 4

He upholds the cause of the oppressed and gives food to the hungry. *Psalm 146:7a (NIV)*

Friday, April 5

The Lord sets prisoners free. *Psalm 146:7b (NIV)*

Saturday, April 6

My soul is in deep anguish. How long, Lord, how long? *Psalm 6:3 (NIV)*

Week 117: April 7-13, 2019

I was also slowly coming to see that there was nothing very passive about Jesus' form of nonviolence, rather his discipleship not only allowed but required the Christian to be actively engaged in the creation of conditions for justice and peace.

Stanley Hauerwas
The Peaceable Kingdom (xxiv)

Sunday, April 7

Speak out for those who cannot speak, for the rights of all the destitute. *Proverbs 31:8 (NRSV)*

Monday, April 8

The nations will see your righteousness, and all kings your glory; and you will be called by a new name which the mouth of the Lord will designate. *Isaiah 62:2 (NASB)*

Tuesday, April 9

Pursue peace with all [people], and the sanctification without which no one will see the Lord. *Hebrews 12:14 (NASB)*

Wednesday, April 10

"For I know the plans that I have for you," declares the Lord, "plans for welfare and not for calamity to give you a future and a hope." *Jeremiah 29:11 (NASB)*

Thursday, April 11

Therefore thus says the Holy One of Israel, ". . . you have rejected this word and have put your trust in oppression and guile, and have relied on them." *Isaiah 30:12 (NASB)*

Friday, April 12

Then all your people will be righteous; they will possess the land forever, the branch of My planting, the work of My hands. *Isaiah 60:21a (NASB)*

Saturday, April 13

The idols speak deceitfully, diviners see visions that lie; they tell dreams that are false, they give comfort in vain. *Zechariah 10:2a (NIV)*

Week 118: April 14-20, 2019

Again and again, story after story, Jesus preaches against economic injustice.

Donald B. Kraybill
The Upside-Down Kingdom (86)

Sunday, April 14 - *Palm Sunday*

Lift up your heads, O gates! and be lifted up, O ancient doors! that the King of glory may come in. *Psalm 24:9 (NRSV)*

Monday, April 15

The people wander like sheep oppressed for lack of a shepherd. *Zechariah 10:2b (NIV)*

Tuesday, April 16

They did not remember his power—the day he redeemed them from the oppressor. *Psalm 78:42 (NIV)*

Wednesday, April 17

Reach down your hand from on high; deliver me and rescue me from the mighty waters. *Psalm 144:7a (NIV)*

Thursday, April 18

Who also brings me out from my enemies; You even lift me above those who rise up against me; You rescue me from the violent man. *2 Samuel 22:49b (NASB)*

Friday, April 19 - *Good Friday*

He was oppressed and He was afflicted, yet He did not open His mouth; like a lamb that is led to slaughter, and like a sheep that is silent before its shearers, so He did not open His mouth. *Isaiah 53:7 (NASB)*

Saturday, April 20 - *Holy Saturday*

Do not be afraid, little flock, for your Father has chosen gladly to give you the kingdom. *Luke 12:32 (NASB)*

Week 119: April 21-27, 2019

It is a caricature of love to try to cover over with alms what is lacking in justice, to patch over with an appearance of benevolence when social justice is missing. True love begins by demanding what is just in the relations of those who love.

Oscar A. Romero
The Violence of Love (130)

Sunday, April 21 - *Easter Sunday*

Behold, I will bring to it health and healing, and I will heal them; and I will reveal to them an abundance of peace and truth. *Jeremiah 33:6 (NASB)*

Monday, April 22

Deliver the person who has been robbed from the power of his oppressor. *Jeremiah 21:12b (NASB)*

Tuesday, April 23

Though you have made me see troubles, many and bitter, you will restore my life again; from the depths of the earth you will again bring me up. *Psalm 71:20 (NIV)*

Wednesday, April 24

I will make a covenant of peace with them and eliminate harmful beasts from the land so that they may live securely in the wilderness and sleep in the woods. *Ezekiel 34:25 (NASB)*

Thursday, April 25

If there is among you anyone in need, a member of your community in any of your towns within the land that the Lord your God is giving you, do not be hard-hearted or tight-fisted toward your needy neighbor. *Deuteronomy 15:7 (NRSV)*

Friday, April 26

He satisfies the thirsty, and the hungry he fills with good things. *Psalm 107:9 (NRSV)*

Saturday, April 27

I know what it is to have little, and I know what it is to have plenty. In any and all circumstances I have learned the secret of being well-fed and of going hungry, of having plenty and of being in need. *Philippians 4:12 (NRSV)*

Week 120: April 28—May 4, 2019

Love is inextricably interwoven with hope and justice.

José Míguez Bonino
Doing Theology in a
Revolutionary Situation (114)

Sunday, April 28

Blessed are those who are persecuted for righteousness' sake, for theirs is the kingdom of heaven. *Matthew 5:10 (NRSV)*

Monday, April 29

If it is possible, as far as it depends on you, live at peace with everyone. *Romans 12:18 (NIV)*

Tuesday, April 30

Thus [God] looked for justice, but behold, bloodshed; for righteousness, but behold, a cry of distress. *Isaiah 5:7b (NASB)*

Wednesday, May 1

Righteousness exalts a nation, but sin is a reproach to any people. *Proverbs 14:34 (NRSV)*

Thursday, May 2

When you reap the harvest of your land, you shall not reap to the very edges of your field, or gather the gleanings of your harvest; you shall leave them for the poor and for the alien: I am the Lord your God. *Leviticus 23:22 (NRSV)*

Friday, May 3

Shall one who hates justice govern? Will you condemn one who is righteous and mighty? *Job 34:17 (NRSV)*

Saturday, May 4

A merchant, in whose hands are false balances, [that one] loves to oppress. *Hosea 12:7 (NASB)*

Week 121: May 5-11, 2019

If the God of Jesus' cross is found among the least, the crucified people of the world, then God is also found among those lynched in American history.

James H. Cone
The Cross and the Lynching Tree (23)

Sunday, May 5

Yes, truth is lacking; and he who turns aside from evil makes himself a prey. Now the Lord saw, and it was displeasing in His sight that there was no justice. *Isaiah 59:15 (NASB)*

Monday, May 6

But when grace is shown to the wicked, they do not learn righteousness; even in a land of uprightness they go on doing evil and do not regard the majesty of the Lord. *Isaiah 26:10 (NIV)*

Tuesday, May 7

Slanderous men have been in [the nation] for the purpose of shedding blood. *Ezekiel 22:9a (NASB)*

Wednesday, May 8

Shall I ransom them from the power of Sheol? Shall I redeem them from death? O Death, where are your thorns? O Sheol, where is your sting? Compassion will be hidden from My sight. *Hosea 13:14 (NASB)*

Thursday, May 9

The Lord also will be a stronghold for the oppressed, a stronghold in times of trouble. *Psalm 9:9 (NASB)*

Friday, May 10

You will eat the fruit of your labor; blessings and prosperity will be yours. *Psalm 128:2 (NIV)*

Saturday, May 11

Scarcely are [the rulers of the earth] planted, scarcely sown, scarcely has their stem taken root in the earth, when he blows upon them, and they wither, and the tempest carries them off like stubble. *Isaiah 40:24 (NRSV)*

Week 122: May 12-18, 2019

It's a profound, mysterious truth—Jesus' concept of love overpowering hate. I may not see its victory in my lifetime. But I know it's true.

John M. Perkins
Let Justice Roll Down (196)

Sunday, May 12

For whatever is born of God overcomes the world; and this is the victory that has overcome the world—our faith. *1 John 5:4 (NASB)*

Monday, May 13

If any who are dependent on you become so impoverished that they sell themselves to you, you shall not make them serve as slaves. *Leviticus 25:39 (NRSV)*

Tuesday, May 14

The Lord has bared His holy arm in the sight of all the nations, that all the ends of the earth may see the salvation of our God. *Isaiah 52:10 (NASB)*

Wednesday, May 15

Evil will not depart from the house of one who returns evil for good. *Proverbs 17:13 (NRSV)*

Thursday, May 16

If he is a poor man, you shall not sleep with his pledge. *Deuteronomy 24:12 (NASB)*

Friday, May 17

Like a muddied spring or a polluted fountain are the righteous who give way before the wicked. *Proverbs 25:26 (NRSV)*

Saturday, May 18

The poor and the oppressor have this in common: the Lord gives light to the eyes of both. *Proverbs 29:13 (NRSV)*

Week 123: May 19-25, 2019

Ideas create outcomes that, if unexamined, reinforce old ideas—
America's oldest idea being that the white race rules. White folks
don't just control America's institutions; they control the narrative.
And the narrative, I believe, controls just about everything else.

Debby Irving
Waking Up White,
and Finding Myself in the Story of Race (67)

Sunday, May 19

The wage of the righteous leads to life, the gain of the wicked to sin. *Proverbs 10:16 (NRSV)*

Monday, May 20

But the Lord is faithful; he will strengthen you and guard you from the evil one. *2 Thessalonians 3:3 (NRSV)*

Tuesday, May 21

Therefore the Lord has kept the calamity in store and brought it on us; for the Lord our God is righteous with respect to all [the] deeds which [God] has done, but we have not obeyed [God's] voice. *Daniel 9:14 (NASB)*

Wednesday, May 22

Finally, brethren, rejoice, be made complete, be comforted, be like-minded, live in peace; and the God of love and peace will be with you. *2 Corinthians 13:11 (NASB)*

Thursday, May 23

[The wicked] are like a lion hungry for prey, like a fierce lion crouching in cover. *Psalm 17:12 (NIV)*

Friday, May 24

They push the needy aside from the road. *Job 24:4a (NASB)*

Saturday, May 25

The poor of the land are made to hide themselves altogether. *Job 24:4b (NASB)*

Week 124: May 26—June 1, 2019

The true measure of our commitment to justice, the character
of our society, our commitment to the rule of law, fairness, and
equality cannot be measured by how we treat the rich, the powerful,
the privileged, and the respected among us. The true measure of
our character is how we treat the poor, the disfavored, the accused,
the incarcerated, and the condemned.

Bryan Stevenson
*Just Mercy: A Story of
Justice and Redemption* (18)

Sunday, May 26

It is I who judge with equity. *Psalm 75:2b (NIV)*

Monday, May 27 - *Memorial Day*

Remember your word to your servant, for you have given me hope.
Psalm 119:49 (NIV)

Tuesday, May 28

They have freely scattered their gifts to the poor, their righteousness
endures forever; their horn will be lifted high in honor
Psalm 112:9 (NIV)

Wednesday, May 29

For there was not a needy person among them, for all who were
owners of land or houses would sell them and bring the proceeds of
the sales. *Acts 4:34 (NASB)*

Thursday, May 30

Your people settled in it, and from your bounty, God, you provided
for the poor. *Psalm 68:10 (NIV)*

Friday, May 31

You have persevered and have endured hardships for my name, and
have not grown weary. *Revelation 2:3 (NIV)*

Saturday, June 1

The words of their mouths are wicked and deceitful; they fail to act
wisely or do good. *Psalm 36:3 (NIV)*

Week 125: June 2-8, 2019

Jesus makes an unqualified identification with the poor and the helpless and takes their pain upon himself.

James H. Cone
The Spirituals and the Blues (49)

Sunday, June 2

Arise, cry out in the night, at the beginning of the watches! Pour out your heart like water before the presence of the Lord! Lift your hands to him for the lives of your children, who faint for hunger at the head of every street. *Lamentations 2:19 (NRSV)*

Monday, June 3

For people who are wicked and deceitful have opened their mouths against me; they have spoken against me with lying tongues. *Psalm 109:2 (NIV)*

Tuesday, June 4

If anyone of your kin falls into difficulty and sells a piece of property, then the next of kin shall come and redeem what the relative has sold. *Leviticus 25:25 (NRSV)*

Wednesday, June 5

They have wronged the poor and needy and have oppressed the sojourner without justice. *Ezekiel 22:29b (NASB)*

Thursday, June 6

Lord, hear my prayer, listen to my cry for mercy; in your faithfulness and righteousness come to my relief. *Psalm 143:1 (NIV)*

Friday, June 7

The Lord watches over the foreigner and sustains the fatherless and the widow, but he frustrates the ways of the wicked. *Psalm 146:9 (NIV)*

Saturday, June 8

Show us your unfailing love, Lord, and grant us your salvation. *Psalm 85:7 (NIV)*

Week 126: June 9-15, 2019

Lamentation is not the opposite of praise but a form of praise in which God is held accountable to God's promises: to comfort the widow and heal the afflicted.

Catherine Mowry LaCugna
God for Us (341)

Sunday, June 9 - *Pentecost Sunday*

And hope does not put us to shame, because God's love has been poured out into our hearts through the Holy Spirit, who has been given to us. *Romans 5:5 (NIV)*

Monday, June 10

The alien who resides with you shall be to you as the citizen among you; you shall love the alien as yourself, for you were aliens in the land of Egypt: I am the Lord your God. *Leviticus 19:34 (NRSV)*

Tuesday, June 11

Show us your unfailing love, Lord, and grant us your salvation. *Psalm 85:7 (NIV)*

Wednesday, June 12

Hear my prayer, Lord, listen to my cry for help; do not be deaf to my weeping. I dwell with you as a foreigner a stranger, as all my ancestors were. *Psalm 39:12 (NIV)*

Thursday, June 13

The wicked borrow and do not repay, but the righteous give generously. *Psalm 37:21 (NIV)*

Friday, June 14

But on the seventh year you shall let [the land] rest and lie fallow, so that the needy of your people may eat; and whatever they leave the beast of the field may eat. You are to do the same with your vineyard and your olive grove. *Exodus 23:11 (NASB)*

Saturday, June 15

Do not be far from me, for trouble is near and there is no one to help. *Psalm 22:11 (NIV)*

Week 127: June 16-22, 2019

For what we are seeing in our nation is not so much a resurgence of racism as a result of what happens when a powerful pro-democracy momentum is slowed, diverted, or temporarily halted in the movement for social transformation. In human society as in other manifestations of nature, there is apparently no real stasis. Either we go forward or we go backward. We cannot stand still.

Vincent Harding
Hope and History (211)

Sunday, June 16

But the people thirsted there for water; and they grumbled against Moses and said, "Why, now, have you brought us up from Egypt, to kill us and our children and our livestock with thirst?" *Exodus 17:3 (NASB)*

Monday, June 17

The earth is the Lord's, and everything in it, the world, and all who live in it. *Psalm 24:1 (NIV)*

Tuesday, June 18

Is there any wrong on my tongue? Cannot my taste discern calamity? *Job 6:30 (NRSV)*

Wednesday, June 19

Shout for joy, O heavens! And rejoice, O earth! Break forth into joyful shouting, O mountains! For the Lord has comforted His people and will have compassion on [the] afflicted. *Isaiah 49:13 (NASB)*

Thursday, June 20

My righteousness is near, My salvation has gone forth, and My arms will judge the peoples; the coastlands will wait for Me, and for My arm they will wait expectantly. *Isaiah 51:5 (NASB)*

Friday, June 21

Above all, clothe yourselves with love, which binds everything together in perfect harmony. *Colossians 3:14 (NRSV)*

Saturday, June 22

I am exceedingly afflicted; revive me, O Lord, according to Your word. *Psalm 119:107 (NASB)*

Week 128: June 23-29, 2019

Jesus rejected hatred because he saw that hatred meant death to the mind, death to the spirit, death to communion with his Father. He affirmed life; and hatred was the great denial.

Howard Thurman
Jesus and the Disinherited (77-78)

Sunday, June 23

You shall give him his wages on his day before the sun sets, for he is poor and sets his heart on it; so that he will not cry against you to the Lord and it become sin in you. *Deuteronomy 24:15 (NASB)*

Monday, June 24

[The unrighteous] justify the wicked for a bribe, and take away the rights of the ones who are in the right! *Isaiah 5:23 (NASB)*

Tuesday, June 25

Surely the righteous will praise your name, and the upright will live in your presence. *Psalm 140:13 (NIV)*

Wednesday, June 26

"Cursed be anyone who moves a neighbor's boundary marker." *Deuteronomy 27:17a (NRSV)*

Thursday, June 27

Deliver me from my enemies, O God. *Psalm 59:1a (NIV)*

Friday, June 28

Be my fortress against those who are attacking me. *Psalm 59:1b (NIV)*

Saturday, June 29

For your name's sake, Lord, preserve my life; in your righteousness, bring me out of trouble. *Psalm 143:11 (NIV)*

Week 129: June 30—July 6, 2019

Wherever the gospel is preached, we must remember that it's good news will make you crazy. The good news of God's kingdom will force you to question social norms. Jesus will put you at odds with the economic and political systems of our world. This gospel will force you to act, interrupting the world as it is in ways that make even pious people indignant.

Emmanuel Katongole
Mirror to the Church (116)

Sunday, June 30

They have repeatedly stumbled; indeed, they have fallen one against another. Then they said, "Get up! And let us go back to our own people and our native land away from the sword of the oppressor." *Jeremiah 46:16 (NASB)*

Monday, July 1

When the righteous triumph, there is great glory. *Proverbs 28:12a (NRSV)*

Tuesday, July 2

When the wicked prevail, people go into hiding. *Proverbs 28:12b (NRSV)*

Wednesday, July 3

O my God, incline Your ear and hear! Open Your eyes and see our desolations and the city which is called by Your name; for we are not presenting our supplications before You on account of any merits of our own, but on account of Your great compassion. *Daniel 9:18 (NASB)*

Thursday, July 4 - *Independence Day*

Pay attention to Me, O My people, and give ear to Me, O My nation; for a law will go forth from Me, and I will set My justice for a light of the peoples. *Isaiah 51:4 (NASB)*

Friday, July 5

And righteousness will abide in the fertile field. *Isaiah 32:16b (NASB)*

Saturday, July 6

[Who are you] that you have forgotten the Lord your Maker, who stretched out the heavens and laid the foundations of the earth, that you fear continually all day long because of the fury of the oppressor, as he makes ready to destroy? But where is the fury of the oppressor? *Isaiah 51:13 (NASB)*

Week 130: July 7-13, 2019

Oppressed people cannot remain oppressed forever. The yearning for freedom eventually manifests itself.

Martin Luther King, Jr.
Where Do We Go from Here:
Chaos or Community? (170)

Sunday, July 7

A generous person will be enriched, and one who gives water will get water. *Proverbs 11:25 (NRSV)*

Monday, July 8

Keep on doing the things that you have learned and received and heard and seen in me, and the God of peace will be with you. *Philippians 4:9 (NRSV)*

Tuesday, July 9

Blessed are you who are poor, for yours is the kingdom of God. *Luke 6:20b (NRSV)*

Wednesday, July 10

Jesus, looking at him, loved him and said, "You lack one thing; go, sell what you own, and give the money to the poor, and you will have treasure in heaven; then come, follow me." *Mark 10:21 (NRSV)*

Thursday, July 11

For You shall break the yoke of their burden and the staff on their shoulders, the rod of their oppressor, as at the battle of Midian. *Isaiah 9:4 (NASB)*

Friday, July 12

Therefore I will not restrain my mouth; I will speak in the anguish of my spirit; I will complain in the bitterness of my soul. *Job 7:11 (NRSV)*

Saturday, July 13

You saw the distress of our ancestors in Egypt and heard their cry at the Red Sea. *Nehemiah 9:9 (NRSV)*

Week 131: July 14-20, 2019

Righteousness includes liberation. Righteousness will never liberate ungodliness to do its thing. Righteousness, both collective and individual, will lift a people above the frustrating effects of ungodliness and give them the will and power to realize their loftiest aspirations.

Carl F. Ellis, Jr.
Free at Last? (190)

Sunday, July 14

Cut off the sower from Babylon and the one who wields the sickle at the time of harvest; from before the sword of the oppressor they will each turn back to his own people and they will each flee to his own land. *Jeremiah 50:16 (NASB)*

Monday, July 15

You shall not take a bribe, for a bribe blinds the eyes of the wise and perverts the words of the righteous. *Deuteronomy 16:19b (NASB)*

Tuesday, July 16

Endow the king with your justice, O God, the royal son with your righteousness. *Psalm 72:1 (NIV)*

Wednesday, July 17

Turn from evil and do good; seek peace and pursue it.
Psalm 34:14 (NIV)

Thursday, July 18

The memory of the righteous is a blessing, but the name of the wicked will rot. *Proverbs 10:7 (NRSV)*

Friday, July 19

Your righteousness, God, reaches to the heavens, you who have done great things. Who is like you, God? *Psalm 71:19 (NIV)*

Saturday, July 20

[Samuel's] sons, however, did not walk in his ways, but turned aside after dishonest gain and took bribes and perverted justice. *1 Samuel 8:3 (NASB)*

Week 132: July 21-27, 2019

When we are uncaring, when we lack compassion, when we are unforgiving, we will always pay the price for it. It is not, however, we alone who suffer. Our whole community suffers, and ultimately our whole world suffers. We are made to exist in a delicate network of interdependence.

Desmond and Mpho Tutu
The Book of Forgiving (19)

Sunday, July 21

The statutes you have laid down are righteous; they are fully trustworthy. *Psalm 119:138 (NIV)*

Monday, July 22

Turn, I pray, let no wrong be done. Turn now, my vindication is at stake. *Job 6:29 (NRSV)*

Tuesday, July 23

Now, behold, the cry of the sons of Israel has come to Me; furthermore, I have seen the oppression with which the Egyptians are oppressing them. *Exodus 3:9 (NASB)*

Wednesday, July 24

Is this not the fast which I choose, to loosen the bonds of wickedness, to undo the bands of the yoke, and to let the oppressed go free and break every yoke? *Isaiah 58:6 (NASB)*

Thursday, July 25

I put on righteousness, and it clothed me; my justice was like a robe and a turban. *Job 29:14 (NRSV)*

Friday, July 26

Why do you spend money for what is not bread, and your wages for what does not satisfy? Listen carefully to Me, and eat what is good, and delight yourself in abundance. *Isaiah 55:2 (NASB)*

Saturday, July 27

The Lord examines the righteous, but the wicked, those who love violence, he hates with a passion. *Psalm 11:5 (NIV)*

Week 133: July 28—August 3, 2019

We are called to play the Good Samaritan on life's roadside; but that will be only an initial act. One day the whole Jericho Road must be transformed so that men and women will not be beaten and robbed as they make their journey through life.

Martin Luther King, Jr.
Where Do We Go from Here:
Chaos or Community? (187)

Sunday, July 28

Look on my affliction and my distress and take away all my sins.
Psalm 25:18 (NIV)

Monday, July 29

Riches do not profit in the day of wrath, but righteousness delivers from death. *Proverbs 11:4 (NRSV)*

Tuesday, July 30

Those who oppress the poor insult their Maker.
Proverbs 14:31a (NRSV)

Wednesday, July 31

Those who are kind to the needy honor [God].
Proverbs 14:31b (NRSV)

Thursday, August 1

His sons favor the poor, and his hands give back his wealth.
Job 20:10 (NASB)

Friday, August 2

Do horses run on rocks? Or does one plow them with oxen? Yet you have turned justice into poison and the fruit of righteousness into wormwood. *Amos 6:12 (NASB)*

Saturday, August 3

In your righteousness, rescue me and deliver me; turn your ear to me and save me. *Psalm 71:2 (NIV)*

Week 134: August 4-10, 2019

One of the crucial insights of the Bible is that God is on the side of justice, that God is concerned for the well-being of those who lack the power to secure it.

Walter Brueggemann
Peace (109-110)

Sunday, August 4

Rise up, O God, judge the earth, for all the nations are your inheritance. *Psalm 82:8 (NIV)*

Monday, August 5

I will take away the chariots from Ephraim and the warhorses from Jerusalem, and the battle bow will be broken. He will proclaim peace to the nations. His rule will extend from sea to sea and from the River to the ends of the earth. *Zechariah 9:10 (NIV)*

Tuesday, August 6

You shall not defraud your neighbor; you shall not steal; and you shall not keep for yourself the wages of a laborer until morning. *Leviticus 19:13 (NRSV)*

Wednesday, August 7

You, O Lord, are enthroned forever; your name endures to all generations. *Psalm 102:12 (NRSV)*

Thursday, August 8

Sell your possessions, and give alms. Make purses for yourselves that do not wear out, an unfailing treasure in heaven, where no thief comes near and no moth destroys. *Luke 12:33 (NRSV)*

Friday, August 9

All day long I have been afflicted, and every morning brings new punishments. *Psalm 73:14 (NIV)*

Saturday, August 10

[Those who would love life] must turn from evil and do good; they must seek peace and pursue it. *1 Peter 3:11 (NIV)*

Week 135: August 11-17, 2019

Love must be interpreted in such a way that it may include condemnation, criticism, resistance and rejection. Within a total biblical view, and in connection with the Kingdom, I think that love must be so reinterpreted.

José Míguez Bonino
*Doing Theology in a
Revolutionary Situation* (122)

Sunday, August 11

Judah has gone into exile with suffering and hard servitude;
she lives now among the nations, and finds no resting place;
her pursuers have all overtaken her in the midst of her distress.
Lamentations 1:3 (NRSV)

Monday, August 12

Proclaim liberty to captives and freedom to prisoners.
Isaiah 61:1c (NASB)

Tuesday, August 13

The hope of the righteous ends in gladness, but the expectation of
the wicked comes to nothing. *Proverbs 10:28 (NRSV)*

Wednesday, August 14

My tongue will tell of your righteous acts all day long, for those
who wanted to harm me have been put to shame and confusion.
Psalm 71:24 (NIV)

Thursday, August 15

Hear, O Lord, and be gracious to me! O Lord, be my helper!
Psalm 30:10 (NRSV)

Friday, August 16

Here is my servant, whom I have chosen, my beloved, with whom
my soul is well pleased. I will put my Spirit upon him, and he will
proclaim justice to the Gentiles. *Matthew 12:18 (NRSV)*

Saturday, August 17

Now this I know: The Lord gives victory to his anointed. He
answers him from his heavenly sanctuary with the victorious power
of his right hand. *Psalm 20:6 (NIV)*

Week 136: August 18-24, 2019

Above all I ask leaders and legislators and the entire international community to confront the reality of those who have been displaced by force, with effective projects and new approaches in order to protect their dignity, to improve the quality of their life, and to face the challenges that are emerging from modern forms of persecution, oppression and slavery. They are human people—I stress this—who are appealing for solidarity and assistance, who need urgent action but, also and above all, understanding and kindness. God is good; let us imitate God.

Pope Francis
The Church of Mercy (105)

Sunday, August 18

There is a conspiracy of her prophets in her midst like a roaring lion tearing the prey. They have devoured lives; they have taken treasure and precious things; they have made many widows in the midst of her. *Ezekiel 22:25 (NASB)*

Monday, August 19

Be merciful, just as your Father is merciful. *Luke 6:36 (NASB)*

Tuesday, August 20

Scoundrels concoct evil, and their speech is like a scorching fire. *Proverbs 16:27 (NRSV)*

Wednesday, August 21

In His name the Gentiles will hope *Matthew 12:21 (NASB)*

Thursday, August 22

The blind receive their sight, the lame walk, the lepers are cleansed, the deaf hear, the dead are raised, and the poor have good news brought to them. *Matthew 11:5 (NRSV)*

Friday, August 23

But the house of Israel says, "The way of the Lord is not right." Are My ways not right, O house of Israel? Is it not your ways that are not right? *Ezekiel 18:29 (NASB)*

Saturday, August 24

You shall not bear a false report; do not join your hand with a wicked man to be a malicious witness. *Exodus 23:1 (NASB)*

Week 137: August 25-31, 2019

If whatever happens in our spiritual lives individually and in community does not have bearing on those who are not counted, then it is not of the Spirit, not of true religion, not pure and single-hearted devotion to the will of God, which wills life, hope, dignity, and abundance for all.

Megan McKenna
Not Counting Women and Children (139)

Sunday, August 25

Whatever house you enter, first say, "Peace to this house!" *Luke 10:5 (NRSV)*

Monday, August 26

The Lord is exalted, for He dwells on high; He has filled Zion with justice and righteousness. *Isaiah 33:5 (NASB)*

Tuesday, August 27

When anguish comes, they will seek peace, but there will be none. *Ezekiel 7:25 (NASB)*

Wednesday, August 28

If I send them away hungry to their homes, they will faint on the way—and some of them have come from a great distance. *Mark 8:3 (NRSV)*

Thursday, August 29

If a brother or sister is without clothing and in need of daily food, and one of you says to them, "Go in peace, be warmed and be filled," and yet you do not give them what is necessary for their body, what use is that? *James 2:15-16 (NASB)*

Friday, August 30

Then Jehoahaz entreated the favor of the Lord, and the Lord listened to him; for He saw the oppression of Israel, how the king of Aram oppressed them. *2 Kings 13:4 (NASB)*

Saturday, August 31

And the peace of God, which surpasses all understanding, will guard your hearts and your minds in Christ Jesus. *Philippians 4:7 (NRSV)*

Week 138: September 1-7, 2019

In order for us as poor and oppressed people to become part of a society that is meaningful, the system under which we now exist has to be radically changed. . . . It means facing a system that does not lend itself to your needs and devising means by which you change that system.

J. Todd Moye
*Ella Baker: Community Organizer of
the Civil Rights Movement* (166)

Sunday, September 1

All the congregation of the Israelites shall be forgiven, as well as the aliens residing among them, because the whole people was involved in the error. *Numbers 15:26 (NRSV)*

Monday, September 2 - *Labor Day*

Therefore, my beloved brethren, be steadfast, immovable, always abounding in the work of the Lord, knowing that your toil is not in vain in the Lord. *1 Corinthians 15:58 (NASB)*

Tuesday, September 3

He has sent me to bind up the brokenhearted. *Isaiah 61:1c (NASB)*

Wednesday, September 4

Better is a little with righteousness than large income with injustice. *Proverbs 16:8 (NRSV)*

Thursday, September 5

Happy are those who do not follow the advice of the wicked, or take the path that sinners tread, or sit in the seat of scoffers. *Psalm 1:1 (NRSV)*

Friday, September 6

So then you are no longer strangers and aliens, but you are fellow citizens with the saints, and are of God's household. *Ephesians 2:19 (NASB)*

Saturday, September 7

My lips will shout for joy when I sing praise to you—I whom you have delivered. *Psalm 71:23 (NIV)*

Week 139: September 8-14, 2019

We are all implicated when we allow other people to be mistreated. An absence of compassion can corrupt the decency of a community, a state, a nation.

Bryan Stevenson
Just Mercy: A Story of
Justice and Redemption (18)

Sunday, September 8

The Sidonians also, and the Amalekites, and the Maonites, oppressed you; and you cried to me, and I delivered you out of their hand. *Judges 10:12 (NRSV)*

Monday, September 9

Israel, put your hope in the Lord both now and forevermore. *Psalm 131:3 (NIV)*

Tuesday, September 10

For the breath of the ruthless is like a rain storm against a wall. *Isaiah 25:4b (NASB)*

Wednesday, September 11

When was it that we saw you a stranger and welcomed you, or naked and gave you clothing? *Matthew 25:38 (NRSV)*

Thursday, September 12

Who will not fear you, Lord, and bring glory to your name? For you alone are holy. All nations will come and worship before you, for your righteous acts have been revealed. *Revelation 15:4 (NIV)*

Friday, September 13

And He came and preached peace to you who were far away, and peace to those who were near. *Ephesians 2:17 (NASB)*

Saturday, September 14

Now this is the account of the forced labor which King Solomon levied to build the house of the Lord, his own house, the Millo, the wall of Jerusalem, Hazor, Megiddo, and Gezer. *1 Kings 9:15 (NASB)*

Week 140: September 15-21, 2019

I raise up my voice—not so I can shout, but so that those without a voice can be heard . . . we cannot succeed when half of us are held back.

Malala Yousafzai
"Speech to the United Nations"

Sunday, September 15

Therefore let it be known to you that this salvation of God has been sent to the Gentiles; they will also listen. *Acts 28:28 (NASB)*

Monday, September 16

The wise are cautious and turn away from evil, but the fool throws off restraint and is careless. *Proverbs 14:16 (NRSV)*

Tuesday, September 17

Woe to you who are full now, for you will be hungry. Woe to you who are laughing now, for you will mourn and weep. *Luke 6:25 (NRSV)*

Wednesday, September 18

Beware that there is no base thought in your heart, saying, "The seventh year, the year of remission, is near," and your eye is hostile toward your poor brother, and you give him nothing; then he may cry to the Lord against you, and it will be a sin in you. *Deuteronomy 15:9 (NASB)*

Thursday, September 19

Do not fear, for I am with you; Do not anxiously look about you, for I am your God. *Isaiah 41:10a (NASB)*

Friday, September 20

Now then let the fear of the Lord be upon you; be very careful what you do, for the Lord our God will have no part in unrighteousness or partiality or the taking of a bribe. *2 Chronicles 19:7 (NASB)*

Saturday, September 21

They said, "You have not defrauded us or oppressed us or taken anything from any man's hand." *1 Samuel 12:4 (NASB)*

Week 141: September 22-28, 2019

We are inevitably our brother's keeper because we are our brother's brother. Whatever affects one directly affects all indirectly.

Martin Luther King, Jr.
Where Do We Go from Here:
Chaos or Community? (181)

Sunday, September 22

O Jerusalem, Jerusalem, the city that kills the prophets and stones those sent to her! How often I wanted to gather your children together, just as a hen gathers her brood under her wings, and you would not have it! *Luke 13:34 (NASB)*

Monday, September 23

From the Lord comes deliverance. May your blessing be on your people. *Psalm 3:8 (NIV)*

Tuesday, September 24

Do not trust in extortion or put vain hope in stolen goods; though your riches increase, do not set your heart on them. *Psalm 62:10 (NIV)*

Wednesday, September 25

Then I will restore your judges as at the first, and your counselors as at the beginning. *Isaiah 1:26a (NASB)*

Thursday, September 26

The righteous gives good advice to friends, but the way of the wicked leads astray. *Proverbs 12:26 (NRSV)*

Friday, September 27

Differing weights are an abomination to the Lord, and false scales are not good. *Proverbs 20:23 (NRSV)*

Saturday, September 28

Vindicate me in your righteousness, Lord my God; do not let them gloat over me. *Psalm 35:24 (NIV)*

Week 142: September 29—October 5, 2019

The perseverance of small, powerless drops of water dripping on the same rock, in the same place, ends by breaking the rock. In the same way, the power of faith with perseverance can break walls of hatred, of rejection, and of violent injustice.

Elias Chacour
We Belong to the Land (207)

Sunday, September 29

You have taken interest and profits, and you have injured your neighbors for gain by oppression, and you have forgotten Me. *Ezekiel 22:12b (NASB)*

Monday, September 30

The righteous will never be removed, but the wicked will not remain in the land. *Proverbs 10:30 (NRSV)*

Tuesday, October 1

And the king will answer them, "Truly I tell you, just as you did it to one of the least of these who are members of my family, you did it to me." *Matthew 25:40 (NRSV)*

Wednesday, October 2

He will revive us after two days; He will raise us up on the third day, that we may live before Him. *Hosea 6:2 (NASB)*

Thursday, October 3

I am the Lord, I have called You in righteousness, I will also hold You by the hand and watch over You, and I will appoint You as a covenant to the people, as a light to the nations. *Isaiah 42:6 (NASB)*

Friday, October 4

To this present hour we are both hungry and thirsty, and are poorly clothed, and are roughly treated, and are homeless. *1 Corinthians 4:11 (NASB)*

Saturday, October 5

Be joyful in hope, patient in affliction, faithful in prayer. *Romans 12:12 (NIV)*

Week 143: October 6-12, 2019

Real change comes from people who make up their minds that if they see something they will do something.

Gwen Ifill
"Commencement Address" at
Wake Forest University

Sunday, October 6

[The Lord] turns rivers into a desert, springs of water into thirsty ground. *Psalm 107:33 (NRSV)*

Monday, October 7

The Lord is close to the brokenhearted and saves those who are crushed in spirit. *Psalm 34:18 (NIV)*

Tuesday, October 8

Pure and undefiled religion in the sight of our God and Father is this: to visit orphans and widows in their distress, and to keep oneself unstained by the world. *James 1:27 (NASB)*

Wednesday, October 9

Then Nebuzaradan the captain of the guard carried away into exile some of the poorest of the people, the rest of the people who were left in the city, the deserters who had deserted to the king of Babylon and the rest of the artisans. *Jeremiah 52:15 (NASB)*

Thursday, October 10

But the poor man had nothing except one little ewe lamb which he bought and nourished; and it grew up together with him and his children. It would eat of his bread and drink of his cup and lie in his bosom, and was like a daughter to him. *2 Samuel 12:3 (NASB)*

Friday, October 11

Peace I leave with you; my peace I give to you. I do not give to you as the world gives. *John 14:27a (NRSV)*

Saturday, October 12

Do not let your hearts be troubled, and do not let them be afraid. *John 14:27b (NRSV)*

Week 144: October 13-19, 2019

Let us resolve to make and keep others free, and let us resist the urge to colonize God for our group's needs.

Charles Marsh
The Beloved Community (213)

Sunday, October 13

Wealth is a ransom for a person's life, but the poor get no threats.
Proverbs 13:8 (NRSV)

Monday, October 14

Restore us, O God; make your face shine on us, that we may be
saved. *Psalm 80:3 (NIV)*

Tuesday, October 15

Truly he is my rock and my salvation; he is my fortress, I will not be
shaken. *Psalm 62:6 (NIV)*

Wednesday, October 16

Lord, confuse the wicked, confound their words, for I see violence
and strife in the city. *Psalm 55:9 (NIV)*

Thursday, October 17

Treat others the same way you want them to treat you.
Luke 6:31 (NASB)

Friday, October 18

You Lord will keep the needy safe and will protect us forever from
the wicked. *Psalm 12:7 (NIV)*

Saturday, October 19

Behold, this was the guilt of your sister Sodom: she and her
daughters had arrogance, abundant food and careless ease, but she
did not help the poor and needy. *Ezekiel 16:49 (NASB)*

Week 145: October 20-26, 2019

We are not expecting utopia here on this earth. But God meant for things to be much easier than we have made them. A man has a natural right to food, clothing, and shelter. A certain amount of goods is necessary to lead a good life. A family needs work as well as bread. Property is proper to man. We must keep repeating these things. Eternal life begins now.

Dorothy Day
On Pilgrimage (177)

Sunday, October 20

I was thirsty and you gave me something to drink. *Matthew 25:35b (NRSV)*

Monday, October 21

So I said, "Wisdom is better than strength." But the wisdom of the poor man is despised and his words are not heeded. *Ecclesiastes 9:16 (NASB)*

Tuesday, October 22

Truly my soul finds rest in God; my salvation comes from him. *Psalm 62:1 (NIV)*

Wednesday, October 23

Surely the righteous will never be shaken; they will be remembered forever. *Psalm 112:6 (NIV)*

Thursday, October 24

When you make a sale to your neighbor or buy from your neighbor, you shall not cheat one another. *Leviticus 25:14 (NRSV)*

Friday, October 25

Leave your orphans behind, I will keep them alive; and let your widows trust in Me. *Jeremiah 49:11 (NASB)*

Saturday, October 26

Woe to you, scribes and Pharisees, hypocrites! For you tithe mint, dill, and cummin, and have neglected the weightier matters of the law: justice and mercy and faith. It is these you ought to have practiced without neglecting the others. *Matthew 23:23 (NRSV)*

Week 146: October 27—November 2, 2019

Each individual Christian and every community is called to be an instrument of God for the liberation and promotion of the poor, and for enabling them to be fully a part of society.

Pope Francis
The Church of Mercy (23)

Sunday, October 27

Do not withhold good from those to whom it is due, when it is in your power to do it. *Proverbs 3:27 (NRSV)*

Monday, October, 28

The Lord said, "Surely I will set you free for purposes of good; surely I will cause the enemy to make supplication to you in a time of disaster and a time of distress." *Jeremiah 15:11 (NASB)*

Tuesday, October 29

If you, even you, had only recognized on this day the things that make for peace! But now they are hidden from your eyes. *Luke 19:42 (NRSV)*

Wednesday, October 30

You shall have a full and just weight; you shall have a full and just measure, that your days may be prolonged in the land which the Lord your God gives you. *Deuteronomy 25:15 (NASB)*

Thursday, October 31

Sing to the Lord, praise the Lord! For He has delivered the soul of the needy one from the hand of evildoers. *Jeremiah 20:13 (NASB)*

Friday, November 1

The righteous have enough to satisfy their appetite, but the belly of the wicked is empty. *Proverbs 13:25 (NRSV)*

Saturday, November 2

For we are sojourners before You, and tenants, as all our fathers were; our days on the earth are like a shadow. *1 Chronicles 29:15a (NASB)*

Week 147: November 3-9, 2019

The resurrection of Jesus is God giving people meaning beyond history, when such violence as slavery and lynching seemed to close off any future.

James H. Cone
The Cross and the Lynching Tree (26)

Sunday, November 3

Sow with a view to righteousness, reap in accordance with kindness; break up your fallow ground, for it is time to seek the Lord until He comes to rain righteousness on you. *Hosea 10:12 (NASB)*

Monday, November 4

And they do not defend the rights of the poor. *Jeremiah 5:28c (NASB)*

Tuesday, November 5 - *Election Day*

Like a roaring lion or a charging bear is a wicked ruler over a poor people. *Proverbs 28:15 (NRSV)*

Wednesday, November 6

Yet because this widow keeps bothering me, I will grant her justice, so that she may not wear me out by continually coming. *Luke 18:5 (NRSV)*

Thursday, November 7

But I pray to you, Lord, in the time of your favor; in your great love, O God, answer me with your sure salvation. *Psalm 69:13 (NIV)*

Friday, November 8

Do not say, "I will repay evil"; wait for the Lord, and he will help you. *Proverbs 20:22 (NRSV)*

Saturday, November 9

So show your love for the alien, for you were aliens in the land of Egypt. *Deuteronomy 10:19 (NASB)*

Week 148: November 10-16, 2019

A society concerned with shalom will care for the most marginalized among them. God has a special concern for the poor and needy, because how we treat them reveals our hearts, regardless of the rhetoric we employ to make ourselves sound just.

Randy S. Woodley
Shalom and the Community of Creation (15)

Sunday, November 10

Little children, make sure no one deceives you; the one who practices righteousness is righteous, just as [Christ] is righteous. *1 John 3:7 (NASB)*

Monday, November 11

Constantly bearing in mind your work of faith and labor of love and steadfastness of hope in our Lord Jesus Christ in the presence of our God and Father. *1 Thessalonians 1:3 (NASB)*

Tuesday, November 12

Give victory with your right hand, and answer me, so that those whom you love may be rescued. *Psalm 108:6 (NRSV)*

Wednesday, November 13

He acts on high those who are lowly, and those who mourn are lifted to safety. *Job 5:11 (NRSV)*

Thursday, November 14

You have been set free from sin and have become slaves to righteousness. *Romans 6:18 (NIV)*

Friday, November 15

For thus says the Lord, "I have heard a sound of terror, of dread, and there is no peace." *Jeremiah 30:5 (NASB)*

Saturday, November 16

Now at this time while the disciples were increasing in number, a complaint arose on the part of the Hellenistic Jews against the native Hebrews, because their widows were being overlooked in the daily serving of food. *Acts 6:1 (NASB)*

Week 149: November 17-23, 2019

While most Americans continue to cherish the illusion that we live in a classless, equal-opportunity society, our courts, our prisons, our public assistance programs, and our schools all tell a different story.

Barbara Brown Taylor
Speaking of Sin (45)

Sunday, November 17

Beloved, you are acting faithfully in whatever you accomplish for the brethren, and especially when they are strangers. *3 John 1:5 (NASB)*

Monday, November 18

Seek the welfare of the city where I have sent you into exile, and pray to the Lord on its behalf; for in its welfare you will have welfare. *Jeremiah 29:7 (NASB)*

Tuesday, November 19

When an alien resides with you in your land, you shall not oppress the alien. *Leviticus 19:33 (NRSV)*

Wednesday, November 20

May he defend the afflicted among the people and save the children of the needy; may he crush the oppressor. *Psalm 72:4 (NIV)*

Thursday, November 21

And the seed whose fruit is righteousness is sown in peace by those who make peace. *James 3:18 (NASB)*

Friday, November 22

The wicked accept a concealed bribe to pervert the ways of justice. *Proverbs 17:23 (NRSV)*

Saturday, November 23

One who is quick-tempered acts foolishly, and the schemer is hated. *Proverbs 14:17 (NRSV)*

Week 150: November 24-30, 2019

I don't know exactly what the new revolution will look like, but as the center of Christianity shifts from the global West to the global South and East, and as Christians in the United States are forced to gauge the success of the church by something other than money and power, I hope it looks like altars transforming into tables, gates transforming into open doors, and cure-alls transforming into healing oils. I hope it looks like a kingdom that belongs not to the rich, but to the poor, not to the triumphant but to the meek, not to the culture warriors but to the peacemakers.

Rachel Held Evans
Searching for Sunday (225-226)

Sunday, November 24

Plead for the widow. *Isaiah 1:17d (NASB)*

Monday, November 25

[The wicked] do not plead the cause, the cause of the orphan, that they may prosper. *Jeremiah 5:28b (NASB)*

Tuesday, November 26

This is my commandment, that you love one another as I have loved you. *John 15:12 (NRSV)*

Wednesday, November 27

Evil will slay the wicked; the foes of the righteous will be condemned. *Psalm 34:21 (NIV)*

Thursday, November 28 - *Thanksgiving Day*

Then say, "Save us, O God of our salvation, and gather us and deliver us from the nations, to give thanks to Your holy name, and glory in Your praise." *1 Chronicles 16:35 (NASB)*

Friday, November 29

"What do you mean by crushing My people and grinding the face of the poor?" declares the Lord God of hosts. *Isaiah 3:15 (NASB)*

Saturday, November 30

Zion will be redeemed with justice and her repentant ones with righteousness. *Isaiah 1:27 (NASB)*

Week 151: December 1-7, 2019

God always thinks with mercy: do not forget this. God always thinks mercifully. He is the merciful Father! God thinks like the father waiting for the son and who goes to meet him when he spots him coming when he is still far off.

Pope Francis
The Church of Mercy (73)

Sunday, December 1 - *First Sunday in Advent*

Yet those who wait for the Lord will gain new strength; they will mount up with wings like eagles, they will run and not get tired, they will walk and not become weary. *Isaiah 40:31 (NASB)*

Monday, December 2

He said to them, "Is it lawful to do good or to do harm on the Sabbath, to save a life or to kill?" *Mark 3:4a (NASB)*

Tuesday, December 3

Behold, a king will reign righteously and princes will rule justly. *Isaiah 32:1 (NASB)*

Wednesday, December 4

I pray that the eyes of your heart may be enlightened, so that you will know what is the hope of [God's] calling, what are the riches of the glory of [God's] inheritance in the saints. *Ephesians 1:18 (NASB)*

Thursday, December 5

But you, Sovereign Lord, help me for your name's sake. *Psalm 109:21a (NIV)*

Friday, December 6

Out of the goodness of your love, deliver me. *Psalm 109:21b (NIV)*

Saturday, December 7

Those who are greedy for unjust gain make trouble for their households, but those who hate bribes will live. *Proverbs 15:27 (NRSV)*

Week 152: December 8-14, 2019

A government that isolates Native Americans on remote reservations sends a message: "You are not wanted." Saturating our culture is the ultimate message: "Belonging to Club America is primarily for white folks."

Debby Irving
Waking Up White,
and Finding Myself in the Story of Race (137)

Sunday, December 8 - *Second Sunday in Advent*

Be still before the Lord and wait patiently for him; do not fret when people succeed in their ways, when they carry out their wicked schemes. *Psalm 37:7 (NIV)*

Monday, December 9

The desire of the righteous ends only in good; the expectation of the wicked in wrath. *Proverbs 11:23 (NRSV)*

Tuesday, December 10

Please, my brothers, do not act wickedly. *Genesis 19:7 (NASB)*

Wednesday, December 11

You shall appoint for yourself judges and officers in all your towns which the Lord your God is giving you, according to your tribes, and they shall judge the people with righteous judgment. *Deuteronomy 16:18 (NASB)*

Thursday, December 12

How boastful you are about the valleys! Your valley is flowing away, O backsliding daughter who trusts in her treasures, saying, "Who will come against me?" *Jeremiah 49:4 (NASB)*

Friday, December 13

And you and the Levite and the alien who is among you shall rejoice in all the good which the Lord your God has given you and your household. *Deuteronomy 26:11 (NASB)*

Saturday, December 14

We have offended you deeply, failing to keep the commandments, the statutes, and the ordinances that you commanded your servant Moses. *Nehemiah 1:7 (NRSV)*

Week 153: December 15-21, 2019

We cannot carry the Gospel to the poor and lowly while emulating the practices of the rich and powerful.

Jen Hatmaker
7 (68)

Sunday, December 15 - *Third Sunday in Advent*

It is good that one should wait quietly for the salvation of the Lord. *Lamentations 3:26 (NRSV)*

Monday, December 16

In the pride of their countenance the wicked say, "God will not seek it out"; all their thoughts are, "There is no God." *Psalm 10:4 (NRSV)*

Tuesday, December 17

It was not by their sword that they won the land, nor did their arm bring them victory; it was your right hand, your arm, and the light of your face, for you loved them. *Psalm 44:3 (NIV)*

Wednesday, December 18

For it would be better for them not to have known the way of righteousness, than having known it, to turn away from the holy commandment handed on to them. *2 Peter 2:21 (NASB)*

Thursday, December 19

They scoff, and speak with malice; with arrogance they threaten oppression. *Psalm 73:8 (NIV)*

Friday, December 20

Scoundrels use wicked methods, they make up evil schemes to destroy the poor with lies, even when the plea of the needy is just. *Isaiah 32:7 (NIV)*

Saturday, December 21

And while being reviled, He did not revile in return; while suffering, He uttered no threats, but kept entrusting Himself to Him who judges righteously. *1 Peter 2:23 (NASB)*

Week 154: December 22-28, 2019

God, is defined in terms of love rather than power.

William C. Placher
Narratives of a Vulnerable God (73).

Sunday, December 22 - *Fourth Sunday in Advent*

Therefore, return to your God, observe kindness and justice, and wait for your God continually. *Hosea 12:6 (NASB)*

Monday, December 23

Is it not to divide your bread with the hungry and bring the homeless poor into the house; when you see the naked, to cover him; and not to hide yourself from your own flesh? *Isaiah 58:7 (NASB)*

Tuesday, December 24 - *Christmas Eve*

O Lord, be gracious to us; we have waited for You. Be their strength every morning, our salvation also in the time of distress. *Isaiah 33:2 (NASB)*

Wednesday, December 25 - *Christmas Day*

"Behold, the tabernacle of God is among [them], and [God] will dwell among them." *Revelation 21:3b (NASB)*

Thursday, December 26

Restore us, God Almighty; make your face shine on us, that we may be saved. *Psalm 80:7 (NIV)*

Friday, December 27

You heard my plea, "Do not close your ear to my cry for help, but give me relief!" *Lamentations 3:56 (NRSV)*

Saturday, December 28

But when you give a reception, invite the poor, the crippled, the lame, the blind, and you will be blessed, since they do not have the means to repay you; for you will be repaid at the resurrection of the righteous. *Luke 14:13-14 (NASB)*

2020

Week 155:
December 29, 2019—January 4, 2020

Our sojourn into the a violent and hurting world is shaped by the memory of the Christ who was born in a stable because there was no room for him at the inn.

Charles Marsh
The Beloved Community (210)

Sunday, December 29

As it is written, "He scattered abroad, he gave to the poor, His righteousness endures forever." *2 Corinthians 9:9 (NASB)*

Monday, December 30

[The Lord] will regard the prayer of the destitute, and will not despise their prayer. *Psalm 102:17 (NRSV)*

Tuesday, December 31

The way of the righteous is smooth; O Upright One, make the path of the righteous level. *Isaiah 26:7 (NASB)*

Wednesday, January 1 - *New Year's Day*

Surely there is a future, and your hope will not be cut off. *Proverbs 23:18 (NRSV)*

Thursday, January 2

They hate the one who reproves in the gate, and they abhor the one who speaks the truth. *Amos 5:10 (NRSV)*

Friday, January 3

If you say, "Look, we did not know this"—does not he who weighs the heart perceive it? Does not he who keeps watch over your soul know it? And will he not repay all according to their deeds? *Proverbs 24:12 (NRSV)*

Saturday, January 4

They trample on the heads of the poor as on the dust of the ground and deny justice to the oppressed. *Amos 2:7a (NIV)*

Week 156: January 5-11, 2020

Theologian James Cone has affirmed that God is on the side of the oppressed. What does this mean? It means that the oppressed, when they resist oppression, are resisting unrighteousness.

Carl F. Ellis, Jr.
Free at Last? (29)

Sunday, January 5

In righteousness you will be established; you will be far from oppression, for you will not fear; and from terror, for it will not come near you. *Isaiah 54:14 (NASB)*

Monday, January 6

He has brought down the powerful from their thrones, and lifted up the lowly. *Luke 1:52 (NRSV)*

Tuesday, January 7

Restore us to yourself, O Lord, that we may be restored; renew our days as of old. *Lamentations 5:21 (NRSV)*

Wednesday, January 8

[God] has remembered his love and his faithfulness to Israel; all the ends of the earth have seen the salvation of our God. *Psalm 98:3 (NIV)*

Thursday, January 9

I have great sorrow and unceasing anguish in my heart. *Romans 9:2 (NIV)*

Friday, January 10

And [Pharaoh] made their lives bitter with hard labor in mortar and bricks and at all kinds of labor in the field, all their labors which they rigorously imposed on them. *Exodus 1:14 (NASB)*

Saturday, January 11

So [God] saved them from the hand of the foe, and delivered them from the hand of the enemy. *Psalm 106:10 (NRSV)*

Week 157: January 12-18, 2020

To speak of love of humanity is meaningless. There is no such thing as humanity. What we call humanity has a name, was born, lives on a street, gets hungry, needs all the particular things we need.

Howard Thurman
Mysticism and the Experience of Love (15)

Sunday, January 12

The Lord is my strength and song, and . . . has become my salvation; [the Lord] is my God, and I will praise Him; my father's God, and I will extol Him. *Exodus 15:2 (NASB)*

Monday, January 13

Furthermore, I have seen under the sun that in the place of justice there is wickedness and in the place of righteousness there is wickedness. *Ecclesiastes 3:16 (NASB)*

Tuesday, January 14

But woe to you Pharisees! For you tithe mint and rue and herbs of all kinds, and neglect justice and the love of God; it is these you ought to have practiced, without neglecting the others. *Luke 11:42 (NRSV)*

Wednesday, January 15

The Almighty—we cannot find . . . [God] is great in power and justice, and abundant righteousness [God] will not violate. *Job 37:23 (NRSV)*

Thursday, January 16

For if you remain silent at this time, relief and deliverance will arise for the Jews from another place and you and your father's house will perish. And who knows whether you have not attained royalty for such a time as this? *Esther 4:14 (NASB)*

Friday, January 17

Light shines on the righteous and joy on the upright in heart. *Psalm 97:11 (NIV)*

Saturday, January 18

[God] raises the poor from the dust. *1 Samuel 2:8a (NASB)*

Week 158: January 19-25, 2020

It is not enough to say, "We must not wage war." It is necessary to love peace and sacrifice for it.

Martin Luther King, Jr.
Where Do We Go from Here:
Chaos or Community? (185)

Sunday, January 19

[God] lifts the needy from the ash heap to make them sit with nobles, and inherit a seat of honor; for the pillars of the earth are the Lord's and [God] set the world on them. *1 Samuel 2:8b (NASB)*

Monday, January 20 - *Martin Luther King Day*

For the Lamb at the center of the throne will be their shepherd; "he will lead them to springs of living water." "And God will wipe away every tear from their eyes." *Revelation 7:17 (NIV)*

Tuesday, January 21

Ho! Everyone who thirsts, come to the waters; and you who have no money come, buy and eat. *Isaiah 55:1a (NASB)*

Wednesday, January 22

Shepherd the flock of God among you, exercising oversight not under compulsion, but voluntarily, according to the will of God; and not for sordid gain, but with eagerness. *1 Peter 5:2 (NASB)*

Thursday, January 23

Surely his salvation is near those who fear him, that his glory may dwell in our land. *Psalm 85:9 (NIV)*

Friday, January 24

So it will be at the end of the age. The angels will come out and separate the evil from the righteous. *Matthew 13:49 (NRSV)*

Saturday, January 25

"[God] pled the cause of the afflicted and needy; then it was well. Is not that what it means to know Me?" declares the Lord. *Jeremiah 22:16 (NASB)*

Week 159: January 26—February 1, 2020

People can *meet* God within their own cultural context but in order to *follow* God, they must cross into other cultures because that's what Jesus did in the incarnation and the cross.

Christena Cleveland
Disunity in Christ (21)

Sunday, January 26

If you see oppression of the poor and denial of justice and righteousness in the province, do not be shocked at the sight; for one official watches over another official, and there are higher officials over them. *Ecclesiastes 5:8 (NASB)*

Monday, January 27

Sing to the Lord a new song, for [God] has done marvelous things; [God's] right hand and . . . holy arm have worked salvation. *Psalm 98:1 (NIV)*

Tuesday, January 28

Remember that you were at that time separate from Christ, excluded from the commonwealth of Israel, and strangers to the covenants of promise, having no hope and without God in the world. *Ephesians 2:12 (NASB)*

Wednesday, January 29

Let my vindication come from you; may your eyes see what is right. *Psalm 17:2 (NIV)*

Thursday, January 30

May my prayer come before you; turn your ear to my cry. *Psalm 88:2 (NIV)*

Friday, January 31

Whoever speaks the truth gives honest evidence, but a false witness speaks deceitfully. *Proverbs 12:17 (NRSV)*

Saturday, February 1

For it was the Father's good pleasure for all the fullness to dwell in Him, through Him to reconcile all things to Himself, having made peace through the blood of His cross; through Him, I say, whether things on earth or things in heaven. *Colossians 1:19-20 (NASB)*

Week 160: February 2-8, 2020

A nation's religion is its life, and as such white Christianity is a miserable failure.

W. E. B. DuBois
The Negro in the South (171)

Sunday, February 2

For the Lord your God is the one who goes with you, to fight for you against your enemies, to save you. *Deuteronomy 20:4 (NASB)*

Monday, February 3

The land shall not be sold in perpetuity, for the land is mine; with me you are but aliens and tenants. *Leviticus 25:23 (NRSV)*

Tuesday, February 4

Arise, Lord, in your anger; rise up against the rage of my enemies. Awake, my God; decree justice. *Psalm 7:6 (NIV)*

Wednesday, February 5

Keep me safe, Lord, from the hands of the wicked; protect me from the violent, who devise ways to trip my feet. *Psalm 140:4 (NIV)*

Thursday, February 6

Woe to him who gets evil gain for his house to put his nest on high, to be delivered from the hand of calamity! *Habakkuk 2:9 (NASB)*

Friday, February 7

My times are in your hands; deliver me from the hands of my enemies, from those who pursue me. *Psalm 31:15 (NIV)*

Saturday, February 8

Then he led away into exile all Jerusalem and all the captains and all the mighty men of valor, ten thousand captives, and all the craftsmen and the smiths. None remained except the poorest people of the land. *2 Kings 24:14 (NASB)*

Week 161: February 9-15, 2020

We can no longer afford to worship the God of hate or bow before the altar of retaliation.

Martin Luther King, Jr.
Where Do We Go from Here:
Chaos or Community? (191)

Sunday, February 9

But some of the poorest people who had nothing, Nebuzaradan the captain of the bodyguard left behind in the land of Judah, and gave them vineyards and fields at that time. *Jeremiah 39:10 (NASB)*

Monday, February 10

Then justice will dwell in the wilderness. *Isaiah 32:16a (NASB)*

Tuesday, February 11

You shall not take vengeance or bear a grudge against any of your people, but you shall love your neighbor as yourself: I am the Lord. *Leviticus 19:18 (NRSV)*

Wednesday, February 12

You, therefore, have no excuse, you who pass judgment on someone else, for at whatever point you judge another, you are condemning yourself, because you who pass judgment do the same things. *Romans 2:1 (NIV)*

Thursday, February 13

You have delivered me from death and my feet from stumbling, that I may walk before God in the light of life. *Psalm 56:13 (NIV)*

Friday, February 14

That you will take up this taunt against the king of Babylon, and say, "How the oppressor has ceased, and how fury has ceased! *Isaiah 14:4 (NASB)*

Saturday, February 15

Make us glad for as many days as you have afflicted us, for as many years as we have seen trouble. *Psalm 90:15 (NIV)*

Week 162: February 16-22, 2020

Over and over, when I ask God why all of these injustices are allowed to exist in the world, I can feel the Spirit whisper to me, "You tell me why we allow this to happen. You are my body, my hands, my feet."

Shane Claiborne
The Irresistible Revolution (65)

Sunday, February 16

He said, "Truly I tell you, this poor widow has put in more than all of them, for all of them have contributed out of their abundance, but she out of her poverty has put in all she had to live on." *Luke 21:3-4 (NRSV)*

Monday, February 17

But whoever has the world's goods, and sees [their] brother in need and closes [their] heart against him, how does the love of God abide in [them]? *1 John 3:17 (NASB)*

Tuesday, February 18

The Lord is my rock, my fortress and my deliverer; my God is my rock, in whom I take refuge, my shield and the horn of my salvation, my stronghold. *Psalm 18:2 (NIV)*

Wednesday, February 19

They come to you as people come, and sit before you as My people and hear your words, but they do not do them, for they do the lustful desires expressed by their mouth, and their heart goes after their gain. *Ezekiel 33:31 (NASB)*

Thursday, February 20

The Lord is my light and my salvation—whom shall I fear? The Lord is the stronghold of my life—of whom shall I be afraid? *Psalm 27:1 (NIV)*

Friday, February 21

Do not let the oppressed retreat in disgrace; may the poor and needy praise your name. *Psalm 74:21 (NIV)*

Saturday, February 22

Why do the wicked renounce God, and say in their hearts, "You will not call us to account"? *Psalm 10:13 (NRSV)*

Week 163: February 23-29, 2020

Keep always before your eyes the example of the Good Shepherd, who came not to be served but to serve, and who came to seek out and save what was lost.

Pope Francis
The Church of Mercy (91)

Sunday, February 23

All these died in faith, without receiving the promises, but having seen them and having welcomed them from a distance, and having confessed that they were strangers and exiles on the earth. *Hebrews 11:13 (NASB)*

Monday, February 24

Yet, O Lord of hosts, You who test the righteous, who see the mind and the heart; let me see Your vengeance on them; for to You I have set forth my cause. *Jeremiah 20:12 (NASB)*

Tuesday, February 25

In arrogance the wicked persecute the poor—let them be caught in the schemes they have devised. *Psalm 10:2 (NRSV)*

Wednesday, February 26 - *Ash Wednesday*

For I am poor and needy, and my heart is wounded within me. *Psalm 109:22 (NIV)*

Thursday, February 27

Do not drag me away with the wicked, with those who do evil, who speak cordially with their neighbors but harbor malice in their hearts. *Psalm 28:3 (NIV)*

Friday, February 28

"They will fight against you, but they will not overcome you, for I am with you to deliver you," declares the Lord. *Jeremiah 1:19 (NASB)*

Saturday, February 29

I love the Lord, for he heard my voice; he heard my cry for mercy. *Psalm 116:1 (NIV)*

Week 164: March 1-7, 2020

The bias of the Bible is toward those who crave justice, even if that means calling order—even royal order—into question. Now, however, at least in American Christianity, we are an affluent people who benefit from the way the cards are currently stacked.

Walter Brueggemann
Peace (113)

Sunday, March 1

But in the seventh year there shall be a sabbath of complete rest for the land, a sabbath for the Lord: you shall not sow your field or prune your vineyard. *Leviticus 25:4 (NRSV)*

Monday, March 2

Then the Israelites cried out to the Lord for help; for he had nine hundred chariots of iron, and had oppressed the Israelites cruelly twenty years. *Judges 4:3 (NRSV)*

Tuesday, March 3

Israel, put your hope in the Lord, for with the Lord is unfailing love and with him is full redemption. *Psalm 130:7 (NIV)*

Wednesday, March 4

It shall come about when they say, "Why has the Lord our God done all these things to us?" then you shall say to them, "As you have forsaken Me and served foreign gods in your land, so you will serve strangers in a land that is not yours." *Jeremiah 5:19 (NASB)*

Thursday, March 5

Thus says the man: I am weary, O God, I am weary, O God. How can I prevail? *Proverbs 30:1b (NRSV)*

Friday, March 6

I am the Lord your God who brought you out of the land of Egypt, to be their slaves no more; I have broken the bars of your yoke and made you walk erect. *Leviticus 26:13 (NRSV)*

Saturday, March 7

But the more they afflicted them, the more they multiplied and the more they spread out, so that they were in dread of the sons of Israel. *Exodus 1:12 (NASB)*

Week 165: March 8-14, 2020

Our image of God must keep growing, expanding, and going deeper, becoming more inclusive of others, especially those we do not esteem, acknowledge, or even notice as worthy of our engagement. They perhaps know or have access to seeing us in a way that we need and are searching for. The answers to our doubts, questions, and hopes lie in others' beliefs, needs, and searching, very rarely our own.

Megan McKenna
Not Counting Women and Children (134)

Sunday, March 8

Blessed are those whose help is the God of Jacob, whose hope is in the Lord their God. *Psalm 146:5 (NIV)*

Monday, March 9

O my threshed people, and my afflicted of the threshing floor! What I have heard from the Lord of hosts, the God of Israel, I make known to you. *Isaiah 21:10 (NASB)*

Tuesday, March 10

You shall not cheat one another, but you shall fear your God; for I am the Lord your God. *Leviticus 25:17 (NRSV)*

Wednesday, March 11

Therefore my heart was glad and my tongue exulted; Moreover my flesh also will live in hope. *Acts 2:26 (NASB)*

Thursday, March 12

He will not break a bruised reed or quench a smoldering wick until he brings justice to victory. *Matthew 12:20 (NRSV)*

Friday, March 13

Though all the peoples walk each in the name of [their] god, as for us, we will walk in the name of the Lord our God forever and ever. *Micah 4:5 (NASB)*

Saturday, March 14

Love does no wrong to a neighbor; therefore, love is the fulfilling of the law. *Romans 13:10 (NRSV)*

Week 166: March 15-21, 2020

Many American Christians do not believe that the pursuit of cross cultural unity is particularly relevant to the faith that is expressed in their pulpits and small group meetings.

Christena Cleveland
Disunity in Christ (157)

Sunday, March 15

[God] delivered us from so great a peril of death, and will deliver us,
[God] on whom we have set our hope. And [God] will yet deliver us.
2 Corinthians 1:10 (NASB)

Monday, March 16

(Samuel) said, "These will be the ways of the king who will
reign over you: he will take your sons and appoint them to his
chariots and to be his horsemen, and to run before his chariots."
1 Samuel 8:11 (NRSV)

Tuesday, March 17

[The king] will take the best of your fields and your vineyards
and your olive groves and give them to his servants.
1 Samuel 8:14 (NASB)

Wednesday, March 18

[The king] will take one tenth of your flocks, and you yourselves will
become his slaves. *1 Samuel 8:17 (NIV)*

Thursday, March 19

And in that day you will cry out because of your king, whom you
have chosen for yourselves. *1 Samuel 8:18a (NRSV)*

Friday, March 20

Do not fear! Stand by and see the salvation of the Lord which [the
Lord] will accomplish for you today. *Exodus 14:13b (NASB)*

Saturday, March 21

My covenant with him was a covenant of life and well-being, which
I gave him; this called for reverence, and he revered me and stood in
awe of my name. *Malachi 2:5 (NRSV)*

Week 167: March 22-28, 2020

There must always be confidence that the effect of truthfulness can be realized in the mind of the oppressor as well as the oppressed. There is no substitute for such faith.

Howard Thurman
Jesus and the Disinherited (60)

Sunday, March 22

The eyes of the Lord are in every place, keeping watch on the evil and the good. *Proverbs 15:3 (NRSV)*

Monday, March 23

The Rock! [God's] work is perfect, for all [God's] ways are just. *Deuteronomy 32:4a (NASB)*

Tuesday, March 24

A God of faithfulness and without injustice, righteous and upright is [God]. *Deuteronomy 32:4b (NASB)*

Wednesday, March 25

Rejoice greatly, Daughter Zion! Shout, Daughter Jerusalem! See, your king comes to you, righteous and victorious, lowly and riding on a donkey, on a colt, the foal of a donkey. *Zechariah 9:9 (NIV)*

Thursday, March 26

Then the righteous will answer him, "Lord, when was it that we saw you hungry and gave you food, or thirsty and gave you something to drink?" *Matthew 25:37 (NRSV)*

Friday, March 27

[The wicked] take away the sheaves from the hungry. *Job 24:10b (NASB)*

Saturday, March 28

You will be enriched in everything for all liberality, which through us is producing thanksgiving to God. *2 Corinthians 9:11 (NASB)*

Week 168: March 29—April 4, 2020

Once the personal history of Jesus, including his death, is made central to the theology of God, then we must conclude that God suffers in Christ.

Catherine Mowry LaCugna
God for Us (301)

Sunday, March 29

Wash yourselves, make yourselves clean; remove the evil of your deeds from My sight. Cease to do evil. *Isaiah 1:16 (NASB)*

Monday, March 30

Then they will cry to the Lord, but [God] will not answer them; [God] will hide [God's] face from them at that time, because they have acted wickedly. *Micah 3:4 (NRSV)*

Tuesday, March 31

Do not hide your face from me in the day of my distress. *Psalm 102:2a (NRSV)*

Wednesday, April 1

Incline your ear to me; answer me speedily in the day when I call. *Psalm 102:2b (NRSV)*

Thursday, April 2

The Lord gives sight to the blind, the Lord lifts up those who are bowed down, the Lord loves the righteous. *Psalm 146:8 (NIV)*

Friday, April 3

Then we cried to the Lord, the God of our fathers, and the Lord heard our voice and saw our affliction and our toil and our oppression. *Deuteronomy 26:7 (NASB)*

Saturday, April 4

Good will come to those who are generous and lend freely, who conduct their affairs with justice. *Psalm 112:5 (NIV)*

Week 169: April 5-11, 2020

Christ's suffering on the cross is the suffering of someone out to win in the struggle with evil, not the suffering of a passive victim.

William C. Placher
Narratives of a Vulnerable God (117)

Sunday, April 5 - *Palm Sunday*

It is better to take refuge in the LORD than to put confidence in princes. *Psalm 118:9 (NRSV)*

Monday, April 6

And they began selling their property and possessions and were sharing them with all, as anyone might have need. *Acts 2:45 (NASB)*

Tuesday, April 7

Love and faithfulness meet together; righteousness and peace kiss each other. *Psalm 85:10 (NIV)*

Wednesday, April 8

This is what the Lord Almighty said: Administer true justice; show mercy and compassion to one another. *Zechariah 7:9 (NIV)*

Thursday, April 9

When you reap the harvest of your land, you shall not reap to the very edges of your field, or gather the gleanings of your harvest. *Leviticus 19:9 (NRSV)*

Friday, April 10 - *Good Friday*

By oppression and judgment He was taken away; and as for His generation, who considered that He was cut off out of the land of the living for the transgression of my people, to whom the stroke was due? *Isaiah 53:8 (NASB)*

Saturday, April 11 - *Holy Saturday*

I will give you thanks, for you answered me; you have become my salvation. *Psalm 118:21 (NIV)*

Week 170: April 12-18, 2020

If this crucified man has been raised from the dead and exalted to be the Christ of God, then what public opinion holds to be the lowliest, what the state has determined to be disgraceful, is changed into what is supreme.

Jürgen Moltmann
The Crucified God (327)

Sunday, April 12 - *Easter Sunday*

I will lift up the cup of salvation and call on the name of the Lord. *Psalm 116:13 (NIV)*

Monday, April 13

In that city there was a widow who kept coming to him and saying, "Grant me justice against my opponent." *Luke 18:3 (NRSV)*

Tuesday, April 14

Then once more you shall see the difference between the righteous and the wicked, between one who serves God and one who does not serve [God]. *Malachi 3:18 (NRSV)*

Wednesday, April 15

The eyes of the Lord are on the righteous, and [God's] ears are attentive to their cry. *Psalm 34:15 (NIV)*

Thursday, April 16

Why do You make me see iniquity, and cause me to look on wickedness? Yes, destruction and violence are before me; strife exists and contention arises. *Habakkuk 1:3 (NASB)*

Friday, April 17

And you pay special attention to the one who is wearing the fine clothes, and say, "You sit here in a good place," and you say to the poor [person], "You stand over there, or sit down by my footstool." *James 2:3 (NASB)*

Saturday, April 18

Beware that wrath does not entice you into scoffing, and do not let the greatness of the ransom turn you aside. *Job 36:18 (NRSV)*

Week 171: April 19-25, 2020

Those who challenge violence and injustice without resort to violence themselves, will have, often enough, a tough time of it. To follow Jesus is to believe that it is worth it that injustice needs to be challenged but that the cycle of violence needs to be broken.

William C. Placher
Narratives of a Vulnerable God (118)

Sunday, April 19

I have seen a wicked and ruthless [one] flourishing like a luxuriant native tree. *Psalm 37:35 (NIV)*

Monday, April 20

You shall divide it by lot for an inheritance among yourselves and among the aliens who stay in your midst, who bring forth [children] in your midst. And they shall be to you as the native-born among the [children] of Israel; they shall be allotted an inheritance with you among the tribes of Israel. *Ezekiel 47:22 (NASB)*

Tuesday, April 21

Let us therefore make every effort to do what leads to peace and to mutual edification. *Romans 14:19 (NIV)*

Wednesday, April 22

Come now, you rich, weep and howl for your miseries which are coming upon you. *James 5:1 (NASB)*

Thursday, April 23

The righteousness of the blameless keeps their ways straight, but the wicked fall by their own wickedness. *Proverbs 11:5 (NRSV)*

Friday, April 24

This is the city to be punished, In whose midst there is only oppression. *Jeremiah 6:6b (NASB)*

Saturday, April 25

And Ruth the Moabitess said to Naomi, "Please let me go to the field and glean among the ears of grain after one in whose sight I may find favor." And she said to her, "Go, my daughter." *Ruth 2:2 (NASB)*

Week 172: April 26—May 2, 2020

Justice without peace tends to fragment and destroy a society. Peace without justice is always shaky and uneasy and never permanent.

Naim Ateek
Justice and Only Justice (140)

Sunday, April 26

The reward for humility and fear of the Lord is riches and honor and life. *Proverbs 22:4 (NRSV)*

Monday, April 27

But surely, God is my helper; the Lord is the upholder of my life. *Psalm 54:4 (NRSV)*

Tuesday, April 28

Live in peace with one another. *1 Thessalonians 5:13b (NASB)*

Wednesday, April 29

You do well if you really fulfill the royal law according to the scripture, "You shall love your neighbor as yourself." *James 2:8 (NRSV)*

Thursday, April 30

Never again will they hunger; never again will they thirst. The sun will not beat down on them, nor any scorching heat. *Revelation 7:16 (NIV)*

Friday, May 1

For thus says the Lord God, "My people went down at the first into Egypt to reside there; then the Assyrian oppressed them without cause." *Isaiah 52:4 (NASB)*

Saturday, May 2

Give to everyone who begs from you. *Matthew 5:42a (NRSV)*

Week 173: May 3-9, 2020

Ours is not a story of bitterness—it is a story of love and the triumphs of the God of love. But it is a story carved out of the realities of violence and poverty, ending not in some sugarcoated sense of brotherly love but the deep conviction that only the power of Christ's crucifixion on the cross and the glory of His resurrection can heal the deep racial wounds in both black and white people in America.

John M. Perkins
Let Justice Roll Down (11)

Sunday, May 3

Do not refuse anyone who wants to borrow from you.
Matthew 5:42b (NRSV)

Monday, May 4

For the Lord is a God of justice; How blessed are all those who long
for [God]. *Isaiah 30:18b (NASB)*

Tuesday, May 5

They have taught their tongue to speak lies. *Jeremiah 9:5b (NASB)*

Wednesday, May 6

Do not take interest in advance or otherwise make a profit
from them, but fear your God; let them live with you.
Leviticus 25:36 (NRSV)

Thursday, May 7

So I have come down to deliver them from the power of the
Egyptians, and to bring them up from that land to a good and
spacious land, to a land flowing with milk and honey, to the place of
the Canaanite and the Hittite and the Amorite and the Perizzite and
the Hivite and the Jebusite. *Exodus 3:8 (NASB)*

Friday, May 8

Let them sing before the Lord for [God] comes to judge the earth.
[God] will judge the world in righteousness and the peoples with
equity. *Psalm 98:9 (NIV)*

Saturday, May 9

Cast your cares on the Lord and he will sustain you; he will never let
the righteous be shaken. *Psalm 55:22 (NIV)*

Week 174: May 10-16, 2020

The suffering of the poor is a sign of everything that contradicts the will of God in history, for their suffering is not simply a matter of accident.

Marilyn J. Legge
Liberation Theology (165)

Sunday, May 10

Listen to my cry, for I am in desperate need; rescue me from those who pursue me, for they are too strong for me. *Psalm 142:6 (NIV)*

Monday, May 11

"It shall come about on that day," declares the Lord of hosts, "that I will break his yoke from off their neck and will tear off their bonds; and strangers will no longer make them their slaves." *Jeremiah 30:8 (NASB)*

Tuesday, May 12

Hear me and answer me. My thoughts trouble me and I am distraught. *Psalm 55:2 (NIV)*

Wednesday, May 13

Ephraim is oppressed, trampled in judgment, intent on pursuing idols. *Hosea 5:11 (NIV)*

Thursday, May 14

If your enemies are hungry, give them bread to eat; and if they are thirsty, give them water to drink. *Proverbs 25:21 (NRSV)*

Friday, May 15

Lord, You will establish peace for us, since You have also performed for us all our works. *Isaiah 26:12 (NASB)*

Saturday, May 16

The peoples will take them along and bring them to their place, and the house of Israel will possess them as an inheritance in the land of the Lord as male servants and female servants; and they will take their captors captive and will rule over their oppressors. *Isaiah 14:2 (NASB)*

Week 175: May 17-23, 2020

Any spirituality that does not lead to engagement in the making of peace, the crafting of nonviolent responses to contemporary events and relationships is not worthy of being called a spirituality.

Megan McKenna
Not Counting Women and Children (204)

Sunday, May 17

Rejoice in the Lord, you who are righteous, and praise his holy name. *Psalm 97:12 (NIV)*

Monday, May 18

Praise be to the Lord, for he has heard my cry for mercy. *Psalm 28:6 (NIV)*

Tuesday, May 19

But God will never forget the needy. *Psalm 9:18a (NIV)*

Wednesday, May 20

The hope of the afflicted will never perish. *Psalm 9:18b (NIV)*

Thursday, May 21

For the Lord has commanded us, "I have placed you as a light for the Gentiles, that you may bring salvation to the end of the earth." *Acts 13:47 (NASB)*

Friday, May 22

But love your enemies, and do good, and lend, expecting nothing in return; and your reward will be great. *Luke 6:35a (NASB)*

Saturday, May 23

Now what will you do in the day of punishment, and in the devastation which will come from afar? To whom will you flee for help? And where will you leave your wealth? *Isaiah 10:3 (NASB)*

Week 176: May 24-30, 2020

In each and every case, resisting the powers of disintegration and division requires seeing the world in a clearer perspective. The real history of the world is not defined by the macho clanking of the war machine; the real history is illuminated by the beloved community of God.

Charles Marsh
The Beloved Community (209)

Sunday, May 24

Also on your skirts is found the lifeblood of the innocent poor. *Jeremiah 2:34a (NASB)*

Monday, May 25 - *Memorial Day*

Remember me, O Lord, when you show favor to your people; help me when you deliver them. *Psalm 106:4 (NRSV)*

Tuesday, May 26

In everything do to others as you would have them do to you; for this is the law and the prophets. *Matthew 7:12 (NRSV)*

Wednesday, May 27

Do not envy the wicked, nor desire to be with them. *Proverbs 24:1 (NRSV)*

Thursday, May 28

When Jesus heard this, he said to him, "There is still one thing lacking. Sell all that you own and distribute the money to the poor, and you will have treasure in heaven; then come, follow me. *Luke 18:22 (NRSV)*

Friday, May 29

Those who walk uprightly fear the Lord, but one who is devious in conduct despises [God]. *Proverbs 14:2 (NRSV)*

Saturday, May 30

I do not hide your righteousness in my heart; I speak of your faithfulness and your saving help. I do not conceal your love and your faithfulness from the great assembly. *Psalm 40:10 (NIV)*

Week 177: May 31—June 6, 2020

Power, when shared, is a relationship that enriches everyone . . .
the great rift is between care and carelessness, justice and injustice,
mercy and mercilessness, compassion and indifference. What
divides us is not difference but sin, oppression, and injustice.

Jean Zaru
"The Bible and the Occupation of Palestine"
in *The Bible and the Palestine/Israel Conflict* (83)

Sunday, May 31 - *Pentecost Sunday*

But as for me, I am filled with power, with the spirit of the Lord, and with justice and might, to declare to Jacob his transgression and to Israel his sin. *Micah 3:8 (NRSV)*

Monday, June 1

I was a stranger and you welcomed me. *Matthew 25:35c (NRSV)*

Tuesday, June 2

For where your treasure is, there your heart will be also. *Luke 12:34 (NASB)*

Wednesday, June 3

We know our iniquities: transgressing and denying the Lord, and turning away from our God, speaking oppression and revolt, conceiving in and uttering from the heart lying words. *Isaiah 59:12b-13 (NASB)*

Thursday, June 4

[The good man] does not commit robbery, but gives his bread to the hungry and covers the naked with clothing. *Ezekiel 18:7b (NASB)*

Friday, June 5

Your wealthy are full of violence; your inhabitants speak lies, with tongues of deceit in their mouths. *Micah 6:12 (NRSV)*

Saturday, June 6

Honor widows who are widows indeed. *1 Timothy 5:3 (NASB)*

Week 178: June 7-13, 2020

If love is the acceptance of the other without regard to one's own well-being, then it contains within itself the possibility of sharing in suffering and freedom to suffer as a result of the otherness of the other.

Jürgen Moltmann
The Crucified God (230)

Sunday, June 7

For God is not a God of confusion but of peace.
1 Corinthians 14:33a (NASB)

Monday, June 8

For the power of the wicked will be broken, but the Lord upholds the righteous. *Psalm 37:17 (NIV)*

Tuesday, June 9

When the tempest passes, the wicked are no more, but the righteous are established forever. *Proverbs 10:25 (NRSV)*

Wednesday, June 10

Those who are most helpless will eat. *Isaiah 14:30a (NASB)*

Thursday, June 11

And the needy will lie down in security. *Isaiah 14:30b (NASB)*

Friday, June 12

God will not do wickedly, and the Almighty will not pervert justice. *Job 34:12 (NRSV)*

Saturday, June 13

Blessed is [the one] who perseveres under trial; for once [they have] been approved, [they] will receive the crown of life which the Lord has promised to those who love Him. *James 1:12 (NASB)*

Week 179: June 14-20, 2020

Revolution—spiritual revolution, not reform or welfare—is the only solution to spiritual bankruptcy.

John M. Perkins
Let Justice Roll Down (101)

Sunday, June 14

The righteousness of the upright saves them, but the treacherous are taken captive by their schemes. *Proverbs 11:6 (NRSV)*

Monday, June 15

Whoever is steadfast in righteousness will live, but whoever pursues evil will die. *Proverbs 11:19 (NRSV)*

Tuesday, June 16

All those who are arrogant are an abomination to the Lord; be assured, they will not go unpunished. *Proverbs 16:5 (NRSV)*

Wednesday, June 17

Behold, I cry, "Violence!" but I get no answer; I shout for help, but there is no justice. *Job 19:7 (NASB)*

Thursday, June 18

The [children] of those who afflicted you will come bowing to you, and all those who despised you will bow themselves at the soles of your feet; and they will call you the city of the Lord, the Zion of the Holy One of Israel. *Isaiah 60:14 (NASB)*

Friday, June 19

Arise, Lord! Deliver me, my God! *Psalm 3:7a (NIV)*

Saturday, June 20

Rescue me, Lord, from evildoers; protect me from the violent. *Psalm 140:1 (NIV)*

Week 180: June 21-27, 2020

If I am afraid to speak the truth lest I lose affection, or lest the one concerned should say, "You do not understand," or because I fear to lose my reputation for kindness; if I put my own good name before the other's highest good, then I know nothing of Calvary love.

Amy Carmichael

If (26)

Sunday, June 21

I was a father to the needy. *Job 29:16a (NRSV)*

Monday, June 22

I championed the cause of the stranger. *Job 29:16b (NRSV)*

Tuesday, June 23

For great is your love toward me; you have delivered me from the depths, from the realm of the dead. *Psalm 86:13 (NIV)*

Wednesday, June 24

For what advantage does the wise man have over the fool? What advantage does the poor man have, knowing how to walk before the living? *Ecclesiastes 6:8 (NASB)*

Thursday, June 25

For when the ear heard, it called me blessed, and when the eye saw, it gave witness of me, because I delivered the poor who cried for help, and the orphan who had no helper. *Job 29:11-12 (NASB)*

Friday, June 26

For [God] has not despised nor abhorred the affliction of the afflicted; nor has [God] hidden His face from [them]; But when [they] cried to [God] for help, [God] heard. *Psalm 22:24 (NASB)*

Saturday, June 27

I sought the Lord, and [the Lord] answered me; [God] delivered me from all my fears. *Psalm 34:4 (NIV)*

Week 181: June 28—July 4, 2020

Frequently the faithfulness of the church has been put to the test the moment believers were asked to follow the path of costly conscientious objection in the face of the world's opposition.

John Howard Yoder
The Politics of Jesus (154)

Sunday, June 28

By the tender mercy of our God, the dawn from on high will break upon us, to give light to those who sit in darkness and in the shadow of death, to guide our feet into the way of peace. *Luke 1:78-79 (NRSV)*

Monday, June 29

Throughout the land that you hold, you shall provide for the redemption of the land. *Leviticus 25:24 (NRSV)*

Tuesday, June 30

Grace to you and peace from God our Father and the Lord Jesus Christ. *1 Corinthians 1:3 (NASB)*

Wednesday, July 1

Yet you say, "The way of the Lord is not right." Hear now, O house of Israel! Is My way not right? Is it not your ways that are not right? *Ezekiel 18:25 (NASB)*

Thursday, July 2

If it is a contest of strength, he is the strong one! If it is a matter of justice, who can summon him? *Job 9:19 (NRSV)*

Friday, July 3

In your majesty ride forth victoriously in the cause of truth, humility and justice; let your right hand achieve awesome deeds. *Psalm 45:4 (NIV)*

Saturday, July 4 - *Independence Day*

May the nations be glad and sing for joy, for you rule the peoples with equity and guide the nations of the earth. *Psalm 67:4 (NIV)*

Week 182: July 5-11, 2020

Do I bend down over someone in difficulty, or am I afraid of getting my hands dirty? Am I closed in on myself and my possessions, or am I aware of those in need of help? Do I look in the eye those seeking for justice, or do I turn my gaze aside to avoid looking them in the eye?

Pope Francis
The Church of Mercy (106-107)

Sunday, July 5

A friend loves at all times, and kinsfolk are born to share adversity. *Proverbs 17:17 (NRSV)*

Monday, July 6

The King is mighty, he loves justice—you have established equity; in Jacob you have done what is just and right. *Psalms 99:4 (NIV)*

Tuesday, July 7

If you meet your enemy's ox or his donkey wandering away, you shall surely return it to him. *Exodus 23:4 (NASB)*

Wednesday, July 8

Therefore because you impose heavy rent on the poor and exact a tribute of grain from them, though you have built houses of well-hewn stone, yet you will not live in them; you have planted pleasant vineyards, yet you will not drink their wine. *Amos 5:11 (NASB)*

Thursday, July 9

I rejoice in following your statutes as one rejoices in great riches. *Psalm 119:14 (NIV)*

Friday, July 10

Grace to you and peace from God our Father and the Lord Jesus Christ. *Philemon 1:3 (NRSV)*

Saturday, July 11

For the mountains may be removed and the hills may shake, but My lovingkindness will not be removed from you. *Isaiah 54:10a (NASB)*

Week 183: July 12-18, 2020

Poverty is not a hazard of fortune or a fact of nature but the result of certain people's greed and injustice. It is intolerable because it contradicts the very purpose of God's mighty act of deliverance—to rescue his people from the slavery of Egypt.

José Míguez Bonino
Doing Theology in a
Revolutionary Situation (112)

Sunday, July 12

So we can say with confidence, "The Lord is my helper; I will not be afraid. What can anyone do to me?" *Hebrews 13:6 (NRSV)*

Monday, July 13

Now faith is the assurance of things hoped for, the conviction of things not seen. *Hebrews 11:1 (NASB)*

Tuesday, July 14

May slanderers not be established in the land; may disaster hunt down the violent. *Psalm 140:11 (NIV)*

Wednesday, July 15

We are afflicted in every way, but not crushed; perplexed, but not despairing. *2 Corinthians 4:8 (NASB)*

Thursday, July 16

And the heavens proclaim his righteousness, for [God] is a God of justice. *Psalm 50:6 (NIV)*

Friday, July 17

O My people! Those who guide you lead you astray and confuse the direction of your paths. *Isaiah 3:12b (NASB)*

Saturday, July 18

Riches do not last forever, nor a crown for all generations. *Proverbs 27:24 (NRSV)*

Week 184: July 19-25, 2020

Let us never forget that the community of Christ exists as a structure with four sides open to the world.

Charles Marsh
The Beloved Community (213)

Sunday, July 19

And I delivered you from the hand of the Egyptians, and from the hand of all who oppressed you, and drove them out before you, and gave you their land. *Judges 6:9 (NRSV)*

Monday, July 20

Also do not mistreat or do violence to the stranger, the orphan, or the widow. *Jeremiah 22:3b (NASB)*

Tuesday, July 21

He will wipe every tear from their eyes. There will be no more death or mourning or crying or pain, for the old order of things has passed away. *Revelation 21:4 (NIV)*

Wednesday, July 22

Wealth and riches are in their houses, and their righteousness endures forever. *Psalm 112:3 (NIV)*

Thursday, July 23

Deliver me from the guilt of bloodshed, O God, you who are God my Savior, and my tongue will sing of your righteousness. *Psalm 51:14 (NIV)*

Friday, July 24

All my enemies will be overwhelmed with shame and anguish; they will turn back and suddenly be put to shame. *Psalm 6:10 (NIV)*

Saturday, July 25

At the same time (King) Asa brutally oppressed some of the people. *2 Chronicles 16:10b (NIV)*

Week 185: July 26—August 1, 2020

Discipleship is quite simply extended training in being dispossessed. To become followers of Jesus means that we must, like him, be dispossessed of all that we think gives us power over our own lives and the lives of others.

Stanley Hauerwas
The Peaceable Kingdom (86)

Sunday, July 26

I will come and proclaim your mighty acts, Sovereign Lord; I will proclaim your righteous deeds, yours alone. *Psalm 71:16 (NIV)*

Monday, July 27

But you are obsessed with the case of the wicked; judgment and justice seize you. *Job 36:17 (NRSV)*

Tuesday, July 28

Consider the ravens, for they neither sow nor reap; they have no storeroom nor barn, and yet God feeds them; how much more valuable you are than the birds! *Luke 12:24 (NASB)*

Wednesday, July 29

Restore to me the joy of your salvation and grant me a willing spirit, to sustain me. *Psalm 51:12 (NIV)*

Thursday, July 30

Do not neglect to show hospitality to strangers, for by this some have entertained angels without knowing it. *Hebrews 13:2 (NASB)*

Friday, July 31

Say among the nations, "The Lord reigns." The world is firmly established, it cannot be moved; he will judge the peoples with equity. *Psalm 96:10 (NIV)*

Saturday, August 1

I must bear the indignation of the Lord, because I have sinned . . . , until [God] takes my side and executes judgment for me. [God] will bring me out to the light; I shall see [God's] vindication. *Micah 7:9 (NRSV)*

Week 186: August 2-8, 2020

Every act of compassion is an act that protests injustice; every act that gives life destroys death.

Megan McKenna
Not Counting Women and Children (159)

Sunday, August 2

If a king judges the poor with equity, his throne will be established forever. *Proverbs 29:14 (NRSV)*

Monday, August 3

Let your heart hold fast my words; keep my commandments, and live. *Proverbs 4:4b (NRSV)*

Tuesday, August 4

So whenever you give alms, do not sound a trumpet before you, as the hypocrites do in the synagogues and in the streets, so that they may be praised by others. Truly I tell you, they have received their reward. *Matthew 6:2 (NRSV)*

Wednesday, August 5

God said to him, "Because you have asked this thing and have not asked for yourself long life, nor have asked riches for yourself, nor have you asked for the life of your enemies, but have asked for yourself discernment to understand justice." *I Kings 3:11 (NASB)*

Thursday, August 6

As for what fell among the thorns, these are the ones who hear; but as they go on their way, they are choked by the cares and riches and pleasures of life, and their fruit does not mature. *Luke 8:14 (NRSV)*

Friday, August 7

[The Lord] regarded their distress when he heard their cry. For their sake he remembered his covenant, and showed compassion according to the abundance of his steadfast love. *Psalm 106:44-45 (NRSV)*

Saturday, August 8

I will make a covenant of peace with them; it will be an everlasting covenant with them. And I will place them and multiply them, and will set My sanctuary in their midst forever. *Ezekiel 37:26 (NASB)*

Week 187: August 9-15, 2020

We should not be romantic about peace. *Shalom* is caused by and requires *intervention that will redistribute power.*

Walter Brueggemann
Peace (106)

Sunday, August 9

And the people will be oppressed, each one by another, and each one by his neighbor. *Isaiah 3:5a (NASB)*

Monday, August 10

Whoever gives to the poor will lack nothing, but one who turns a blind eye will get many a curse. *Proverbs 28:27 (NRSV)*

Tuesday, August 11

The upright see it and are glad, and all wickedness stops its mouth. *Psalm 107:42 (NRSV)*

Wednesday, August 12

The hungry eat their harvest, and they take it even out of the thorns; and the thirsty pant after their wealth. *Job 5:5 (NRSV)*

Thursday, August 13

The righteous cry out, and the Lord hears them; he delivers them from all their troubles. *Psalm 34:17 (NIV)*

Friday, August 14

Drip down, O heavens, from above, and let the clouds pour down righteousness. *Isaiah 45:8a (NASB)*

Saturday, August 15

The iniquities of the wicked ensnare them, and they are caught in the toils of their sin. *Proverbs 5:22 (NRSV)*

Week 188: August 16-22, 2020

Society will be just, and in a certain sense new, to the degree that it places the dignity of the human person at its center—a dignity that for a Christian has its ultimate foundation in the condition of being the "image of God" which Christ saves by reestablishing the friendship between human beings and God.

Gustavo Gutiérrez
Gustavo Gutiérrez: Essential Writings (273)

Sunday, August 16

The Lord does not let the righteous go hungry, but he thwarts the craving of the wicked. *Proverbs 10:3 (NRSV)*

Monday, August 17

Yet have regard to the prayer of Your servant and to his supplication, O Lord my God, to listen to the cry and to the prayer which Your servant prays before You. *2 Chronicles 6:19 (NASB)*

Tuesday, August 18

But as for me, afflicted and in pain—may your salvation, God, protect me. *Psalm 69:29 (NIV)*

Wednesday, August 19

[I was] naked and you did not give me clothing. *Matthew 25:43b (NRSV)*

Thursday, August 20

[God] permitted no man to oppress them, and [God] reproved kings for their sakes. *1 Chronicles 16:21 (NASB)*

Friday, August 21

They will not labor in vain, or bear children for calamity; for they are the offspring of those blessed by the Lord, and their descendants with them. *Isaiah 65:23 (NASB)*

Saturday, August 22

Go and learn what this means, "I desire mercy, not sacrifice." For I have come to call not the righteous but sinners. *Matthew 9:13 (NRSV)*

Week 189: August 23-29, 2020

In the face of oppression and darkness, the light is growing brighter, and we are on that side.

Sarah Bessey
Jesus Feminist (152)

Sunday, August 23

Hear my cry for mercy as I call to you for help, as I lift up my hands toward your Most Holy Place. *Psalm 28:2 (NIV)*

Monday, August 24

But to the wicked person, God says: "What right have you to recite my laws or take my covenant on your lips?" *Psalm 50:16 (NIV)*

Tuesday, August 25

A false balance is an abomination to the Lord,
but an accurate weight is his delight. *Proverbs 11:1 (NRSV)*

Wednesday, August 26

For he will deliver the needy who cry out, the afflicted who have no one to help. *Psalm 72:12 (NIV)*

Thursday, August 27

Righteousness belongs to You, O Lord, but to us open shame, as it is this day—to the [people] of Judah, the inhabitants of Jerusalem and all Israel, those who are nearby and those who are far away in all the countries to which You have driven them, because of their unfaithful deeds which they have committed against You. *Daniel 9:7 (NASB)*

Friday, August 28

No one sues righteously and no one pleads honestly. *Isaiah 59:4a (NASB)*

Saturday, August 29

They trust in confusion and speak lies. *Isaiah 59:4b (NASB)*

Week 190: August 30—September 5, 2020

If the present chasm of hostility, fear and distrust is to be bridged, the white man must begin to walk in the pathways of his black brothers and feel some of the pain and hurt that throb without letup in their daily lives.

Martin Luther King, Jr.
Where Do We Go from Here:
Chaos or Community? (102)

Sunday, August 30

They conceive mischief and bring forth iniquity. *Isaiah 59:4c (NASB)*

Monday, August 31

All day long they twist my words; all their schemes are for my ruin. *Psalm 56:5 (NIV)*

Tuesday, September 1

A little while, and the wicked will be no more; though you look for them, they will not be found. *Psalm 37:10 (NIV)*

Wednesday, September 2

[The one] who lends money to the poor without interest; who does not accept a bribe against the innocent. Whoever does these things will never be shaken. *Psalm 15:5 (NIV)*

Thursday, September 3

Then [Jesus] said to them, "Beware, and be on your guard against every form of greed; for not even when one has an abundance does . . . life consist of . . . possessions." *Luke 12:15 (NASB)*

Friday, September 4

Proclaim on the citadels in Ashdod and on the citadels in the land of Egypt and say, "Assemble yourselves on the mountains of Samaria and see the great tumults within her and the oppressions in her midst." *Amos 3:9 (NASB)*

Saturday, September 5

The foot will trample it, the feet of the afflicted, the steps of the helpless. *Isaiah 26:6 (NASB)*

Week 191: September 6-12, 2020

It may not be too much to claim that the future of our world will depend on how we deal with identity and difference.

Miroslav Volf
Exclusion and Embrace (20)

Sunday, September 6

My God, I cry out by day, but you do not answer, by night, but I find no rest. *Psalm 22:2 (NIV)*

Monday, September 7 - *Labor Day*

Come to me, all you that are weary and are carrying heavy burdens, and I will give you rest. *Matthew 11:28 (NRSV)*

Tuesday, September 8

By this everyone will know that you are my disciples, if you have love for one another. *John 13:35 (NRSV)*

Wednesday, September 9

The wicked are overthrown and are no more. *Proverbs 12:7a (NRSV)*

Thursday, September 10

The house of the righteous will stand. *Proverbs 12:7b (NRSV)*

Friday, September 11

May those who delight in my vindication shout for joy and gladness; may they always say, "The Lord be exalted, who delights in the well-being of his servant." *Psalm 35:27 (NIV)*

Saturday, September 12

All one's ways may be pure in one's own eyes, but the Lord weighs the spirit. *Proverbs 16:2 (NRSV)*

Week 192: September 13-19, 2020

From Aboriginal activist work in Queensland in 1970s regarding a theology of "with-ness": If you have come to help me, you are wasting your time. But if you have come because your liberation is bound up with mine, then let us work together.

Scott A. Bessenecker
*Living Mission: The Vision and
Voices of New Friars* (150)

Sunday, September 13

Do not rejoice when your enemies fall, and do not let your heart be glad when they stumble. *Proverbs 24:17 (NRSV)*

Monday, September 14

For consider Him who has endured such hostility by sinners against Himself, so that you will not grow weary and lose heart. *Hebrews 12:3 (NASB)*

Tuesday, September 15

The scepter of the wicked will not remain over the land allotted to the righteous, for then the righteous might use their hands to do evil. *Psalm 125:3 (NIV)*

Wednesday, September 16

Blessed are those who mourn, for they will be comforted. *Matthew 5:4 (NRSV)*

Thursday, September 17

I am for peace; but when I speak, they are for war. *Psalm 120:7 (NIV)*

Friday, September 18

They have greatly oppressed me from my youth, but they have not gained the victory over me. *Psalm 129:2 (NIV)*

Saturday, September 19

In the path of righteousness there is life, in walking its path there is no death. *Proverbs 12:28 (NRSV)*

Week 193: September 20-26, 2020

For a compassionate [person] nothing human is alien; no joy and no
sorrow, no way of living and no way of dying.

Henri Nouwen
The Wounded Healer (41)

Sunday, September 20

Woe to those who enact evil statutes and to those who constantly record unjust decisions. *Isaiah 10:1 (NASB)*

Monday, September 21

I have done what is righteous and just; do not leave me to my oppressors. *Psalm 119:121 (NIV)*

Tuesday, September 22

Deliver me, my God, from the hand of the wicked, from the grasp of those who are evil and cruel. *Psalm 71:4 (NIV)*

Wednesday, September 23

I have seen [their] ways, but I will heal [them]; I will lead [them] and restore comfort to [them]. *Isaiah 57:18 (NASB)*

Thursday, September 24

You shall not wrong a stranger or oppress [them], for you were strangers in the land of Egypt. *Exodus 22:21 (NASB)*

Friday, September 25

Justice is turned back. *Isaiah 59:14a (NASB)*

Saturday, September 26

I will be swift to bear witness . . . against those who swear falsely. *Malachi 3:5a (NRSV)*

Week 194: September 27—October 3, 2020

To say scripture is fulfilled [in Christ] is to take a stand for justice and to struggle to confront injustice, racism, violence, discrimination, and everything that corrupts and dehumanizes people.

Naim Ateek
The Bible and the Palestine/Israel Conflict (36-37)

Sunday, September 27

I will be swift to bear witness against . . . those who oppress the hired workers in their wages. *Malachi 3:5b (NRSV)*

Monday, September 28

I will be swift to bear witness against . . . those who oppress . . . the widow and the orphan. *Malachi 3:5c (NRSV)*

Tuesday, September 29

I will be swift to bear witness against . . . those who thrust aside the alien, and do not fear me, says the Lord of hosts. *Malachi 3:5d (NRSV)*

Wednesday, September 30

Does God pervert justice? *Job 8:3a (NRSV)*

Thursday, October 1

Or does the Almighty pervert the right? *Job 8:3b (NRSV)*

Friday, October 2

On the day that you stood aside, on the day that strangers carried off his wealth, and foreigners entered his gates and cast lots for Jerusalem, you too were like one of them. *Obadiah 1:11(NRSV)*

Saturday, October 3

Do not bring your servant into judgment, for no one living is righteous before you. *Psalm 143:2 (NIV)*

Week 195: October 4-10, 2020

To love is the profoundest act of religion, of religious faith, of religious devotion.

Howard Thurman
Mysticism and the Experience of Love (22)

Sunday, October 4

Come, let us shout for joy to the Lord. *Psalm 95:1a (NIV)*

Monday, October 5

Let us shout aloud to the Rock of our salvation. *Psalm 95:1b (NIV)*

Tuesday, October 6

For what does a man get in all his labor and in his striving with which he labors under the sun? *Ecclesiastes 2:22 (NASB)*

Wednesday, October 7

In you they have taken bribes to shed blood. *Ezekiel 22:12a (NASB)*

Thursday, October 8

[God] will judge between the nations and will settle disputes for many peoples. They will beat their swords into plowshares and their spears into pruning hooks. Nation will not take up sword against nation, nor will they train for war anymore. *Isaiah 2:4 (NIV)*

Friday, October 9

Judgment will again be founded on righteousness, and all the upright in heart will follow it. *Psalm 94:15 (NIV)*

Saturday, October 10

The Lord helps them and delivers them. *Psalm 37:40a (NIV)*

Week 196: October 11-17, 2020

My whole life so far, my whole experience has been that our failure has been not to love enough.

Dorothy Day
On Pilgrimage (126)

Sunday, October 11

[The Lord] delivers them from the wicked and saves them, because they take refuge in [God]. *Psalm 37:40b (NIV)*

Monday, October 12

Those who mislead the upright into evil ways will fall into pits of their own making. *Proverbs 28:10a (NRSV)*

Tuesday, October 13

They only asked us to remember the poor—the very thing I also was eager to do. *Galatians 2:10 (NASB)*

Wednesday, October 14

We hope for light, but behold, darkness, for brightness, but we walk in gloom. *Isaiah 59:9b (NASB)*

Thursday, October 15

Hear this, you who trample the needy, to do away with the humble of the land. . . . "Behold, days are coming," declares the Lord God, "When I will send a famine on the land, not a famine for bread or a thirst for water, but rather for hearing the words of the Lord." *Amos 8:4, 11 (NASB)*

Friday, October 16

Do not plan harm against your neighbor who lives trustingly beside you. *Proverbs 3:29 (NRSV)*

Saturday, October 17

The righteous are delivered from trouble, and the wicked get into it instead. *Proverbs 11:8 (NRSV)*

Week 197: October 18-24, 2020

We offer truth best not by pontificating pronouncements or political maneuverings, but by simply speaking and living truly.

Marva J. Dawn
*Powers, Weakness, and
the Tabernacling of God* (136)

Sunday, October 18

I was a stranger and you did not welcome me.
Matthew 25:43a (NRSV)

Monday, October 19

"Woe to the shepherds who are destroying and scattering the sheep of My pasture!" declares the Lord. *Jeremiah 23:1 (NASB)*

Tuesday, October 20

Let those who love the Lord hate evil, for [God] guards the lives of [the] faithful . . . and delivers them from the hand of the wicked. *Psalm 97:10 (NIV)*

Wednesday, October 21

My whole being will exclaim "Who is like you Lord? You rescue the poor from those too strong for them, the poor and needy from those who rob them." *Psalm 35:10 (NIV)*

Thursday, October 22

For the Lord will not reject his people; he will never forsake his inheritance. *Psalm 94:14 (NIV)*

Friday, October 23

So give for alms those things that are within; and see, everything will be clean for you. *Luke 11:41 (NRSV)*

Saturday, October 24

The people of the land have practiced oppression and committed robbery. *Ezekiel 22:29a (NASB)*

Week 198: October 25-31, 2020

Behavior pleasing to God makes a simple claim: caring for the lonely and the poor and being a people attentive to the "fatherless and the widow in their affliction." Let us throw ourselves into humdrum tasks and the ordinary work of mercy and justice.

Charles Marsh
The Beloved Community (213)

Sunday, October 25

All the days of the poor are hard, but a cheerful heart has a continual feast. *Proverbs 15:15 (NRSV)*

Monday, October, 26

[The scribes] devour widows' houses and for the sake of appearance say long prayers. They will receive the greater condemnation. *Mark 12:40 (NRSV)*

Tuesday, October 27

The sacrifice of the wicked is an abomination; how much more when brought with evil intent. *Proverbs 21:27 (NRSV)*

Wednesday, October 28

They crush olives among the terraces; they tread the winepresses, yet suffer thirst *Job 24:11 (NIV)*

Thursday, October 29

You cannot serve God and wealth. *Matthew 6:24b (NRSV)*

Friday, October 30

But I said, "I have toiled in vain, I have spent My strength for nothing and vanity; yet surely the justice due to Me is with the Lord, and My reward with My God." *Isaiah 49:4 (NASB)*

Saturday, October 31

I was hungry and you gave me no food. *Matthew 25:42a (NRSV)*

Week 199: November 1-7, 2020

Hatred cannot be controlled once it is set in motion.

Howard Thurman
Jesus and the Disinherited (76)

Sunday, November 1

For they sow the wind and they reap the whirlwind. The standing grain has no heads; It yields no grain. Should it yield, strangers would swallow it up. *Hosea 8:7 (NASB)*

Monday, November 2

But the meek will inherit the land and enjoy peace and prosperity. *Psalm 37:11 (NIV)*

Tuesday, November 3 - *Election Day*

Whoever is wise, let him understand these things; whoever is discerning, let him know them. For the ways of the Lord are right, and the righteous will walk in them, but transgressors will stumble in them. *Hosea 14:9 (NASB)*

Wednesday, November 4

Those who trust in their riches will wither, but the righteous will flourish like green leaves. *Proverbs 11:28 (NRSV)*

Thursday, November 5

It will become a sign and a witness to the Lord of hosts in the land of Egypt; for they will cry to the Lord because of oppressors, and [God] will send them a Savior and a Champion, and [God] will deliver them. *Isaiah 19:20 (NASB)*

Friday, November 6

As a partridge that hatches eggs which it has not laid, so is he who makes a fortune, but unjustly; in the midst of his days it will forsake him, and in the end he will be a fool. *Jeremiah 17:11 (NASB)*

Saturday, November 7

The Spirit of the Lord is upon me, because [God] has anointed me to bring good news to the poor. *Luke 4:18a (NRSV)*

Week 200: November 8-14, 2020

Can we be true Christians without being considered to be subversives in the eyes of the oppressors?

Henri Nouwen
¡Gracias! (29)

Sunday, November 8

Now this I say, [the one] who sows sparingly will also reap sparingly, and [the one] who sows bountifully will also reap bountifully. *2 Corinthians 9:6 (NASB)*

Monday, November 9

O grant us help against the foe, for human help is worthless. *Psalm 108:12 (NRSV)*

Tuesday, November 10

You shall not afflict any widow or orphan. *Exodus 22:22 (NASB)*

Wednesday, November 11

He has sent me to proclaim release to the captives and recovery of sight to the blind, to let the oppressed go free. *Luke 4:18b (NRSV)*

Thursday, November 12

[The scribes] devour widows' houses and for the sake of appearance say long prayers. They will receive the greater condemnation. *Luke 20:47 (NRSV)*

Friday, November 13

But the LORD Almighty will be exalted by his justice, and the holy God will be proved holy by his righteous acts. *Isaiah 5:16 (NIV)*

Saturday, November 14

Break the arm of the wicked and evildoers; seek out their wickedness until you find none. *Psalm 10:15 (NRSV)*

Week 201: November 15-21, 2020

If Western civilization does not now respond constructively to the challenge to banish racism, some future historian will have to say that a great civilization died because it lacked the soul and commitment to make justice a reality for all men.

Martin Luther King, Jr.
Where Do We Go from Here:
Chaos or Community? (176)

Sunday, November 15

You shall not cheat in measuring length, weight, or quantity. *Leviticus 19:35 (NRSV)*

Monday, November 16

They weary themselves committing iniquity. *Jeremiah 9:5c (NASB)*

Tuesday, November 17

Then you will call, and the Lord will answer; you will cry, and [God] will say, "Here I am." If you remove the yoke from your midst, the pointing of the finger and speaking wickedness. . . . *Isaiah 58:9 (NASB)*

Wednesday, November 18

I know your afflictions and your poverty—yet you are rich! *Revelation 2:9a (NIV)*

Thursday, November 19

Consider the lilies, how they grow: they neither toil nor spin; but I tell you, not even Solomon in all his glory clothed himself like one of these. But if God so clothes the grass in the field, which is alive today and tomorrow is thrown into the furnace, how much more will [God] clothe you? *Luke 12:27-28 (NASB)*

Friday, November 20

Go out into the highways and along the hedges, and compel them to come in, so that my house may be filled. *Luke 14:23 (NASB)*

Saturday, November 21

Those who counsel peace have joy. *Proverbs 12:20b (NRSV)*

Week 202: November 22-28, 2020

Only the suffering God can help.

Dietrich Bonhoeffer
Letters and Papers from Prison (479)

Sunday, November 22

You shall remember that you were a slave in Egypt, and you shall be careful to observe these statutes. *Deuteronomy 16:12 (NASB)*

Monday, November 23

Deceit is in the mind of those who plan evil. *Proverbs 12:20a (NRSV)*

Tuesday, November 24

Who will rise up for me against the wicked? Who will take a stand for me against evildoers? *Psalm 94:16 (NIV)*

Wednesday, November 25

But, O Lord of hosts, who judges righteously, who tries the feelings and the heart, let me see Your vengeance on them, for to You have I committed my cause. *Jeremiah 11:20 (NASB)*

Thursday, November 26 - *Thanksgiving Day*

But may the righteous be glad and rejoice before God; may they be happy and joyful. *Psalm 68:3 (NIV)*

Friday, November 27

Do not envy the violent and do not choose any of their ways. *Proverbs 3:31 (NRSV)*

Saturday, November 28

He will rescue them from oppression and violence, for precious is their blood in his sight. *Psalm 72:14 (NIV)*

Week 203:
November 29—December 5, 2020

The practice of justice is at the center of God's purpose for human life. It is so closely related to the worship of the living God as the only true God that no act of worship is acceptable to him unless it is accompanied by concrete acts of justice on the human level.

C. Rene Padilla
"God's Call to Do Justice,"
in *The Justice Project* (23)

Sunday, November 29 - *First Sunday in Advent*

[God] will not be disheartened or crushed until . . . justice [is established] in the earth; and the coastlands will wait expectantly for [God's] law. *Isaiah 42:4 (NASB)*

Monday, November 30

The Lord watches over the way of the righteous, but the way of the wicked will perish. *Psalm 1:6 (NRSV)*

Tuesday, December 1

And you shall rejoice before the Lord your God, you and your son and your daughter and your male and female servants and the Levite who is in your town, and the stranger and the orphan and the widow who are in your midst, in the place where the Lord your God chooses to establish His name. *Deuteronomy 16:11 (NASB)*

Wednesday, December 2

Let their lying lips be silenced, for with pride and contempt they speak arrogantly against the righteous. *Psalm 31:18 (NIV)*

Thursday, December 3

Evil plans are an abomination to the Lord, but gracious words are pure. *Proverbs 15:26 (NRSV)*

Friday, December 4

Do not remove an ancient landmark or encroach on the fields of orphans. *Proverbs 23:10 (NRSV)*

Saturday, December 5

Hear this word, you cows of Bashan who are on the mountain of Samaria, who oppress the poor, who crush the needy, who say to your husbands, "Bring now, that we may drink!" The Lord God has sworn . . . "Behold, the days are coming upon you when they will take you away with meat hooks, and the last of you with fish hooks." *Amos 4:1-2 (NASB)*

Week 204: December 6-12, 2020

Love is the motive, but justice is the instrument.

Reinhold Niebuhr
in "James Baldwin and Reinhold Niebuhr: Responsibility,"
Christianity and Crisis (452)

Sunday, December 6 - *Second Sunday in Advent*

I long for your salvation, Lord, and your law gives me delight. *Psalm 119:174 (NIV)*

Monday, December 7

He said, "O man of high esteem, do not be afraid. Peace be with you; take courage and be courageous!" Now as soon as he spoke to me, I received strength and said, "May my lord speak, for you have strengthened me." *Daniel 10:19 (NASB)*

Tuesday, December 8

Therefore love truth and peace. *Zechariah 8:19b (NIV)*

Wednesday, December 9

The Lord said, "I have surely seen the affliction of My people who are in Egypt, and have given heed to their cry because of their taskmasters, for I am aware of their sufferings." *Exodus 3:7 (NASB)*

Thursday, December 10

But I say to you who hear, love your enemies, do good to those who hate you. *Luke 6:27 (NASB)*

Friday, December 11

Seek the Lord that you may live, or [God] will break forth like a fire, O house of Joseph, and it will consume with none to quench it for Bethel, for those who turn justice into wormwood and cast righteousness down to the earth. *Amos 5:6-7 (NASB)*

Saturday, December 12

In peace I will lie down and sleep, for you alone, Lord, make me dwell in safety. *Psalm 4:8 (NIV)*

Week 205: December 13-19, 2020

The God of saving history is the same God from all eternity, and the God of our future.

Catherine Mowry LaCugna
God for Us (348)

Sunday, December 13 - *Third Sunday in Advent*

And will not God grant justice to his chosen ones who cry to him day and night? Will he delay long in helping them? *Luke 18:7 (NRSV)*

Monday, December 14

Then I heard a loud voice in heaven say: "Now have come the salvation and the power and the kingdom of our God, and the authority of his Messiah. For the accuser of our brothers and sisters, who accuses them before our God day and night, has been hurled down." *Revelation 12:10 (NIV)*

Tuesday, December 15

"My covenant of peace will not be shaken," says the Lord who has compassion on you. *Isaiah 54:10b (NASB)*

Wednesday, December 16

The wicked draw the sword and bend the bow to bring down the poor and needy, to slay those whose ways are upright. *Psalm 37:14 (NIV)*

Thursday, December 17

There will be no end to the increase of His government or of peace, on the throne of David and over his kingdom, to establish it and to uphold it with justice and righteousness from then on and forevermore. The zeal of the Lord of hosts will accomplish this. *Isaiah 9:7 (NASB)*

Friday, December 18

He said to them, "If any of you has a sheep and it falls into a pit on the Sabbath, will you not take hold of it and lift it out? How much more valuable is a person than a sheep! Therefore it is lawful to do good on the Sabbath." *Matthew 12:11-12 (NIV)*

Saturday, December 19

I am feeble and utterly crushed; I groan in anguish of heart. *Psalm 38:8 (NIV)*

Week 206: December 20-26, 2020

The spirituals, gospel songs and hymns focused on how Jesus achieved salvation for the least through his solidarity with them even unto death.

James H. Cone
The Cross and the Lynching Tree (20).

Sunday, December 20 - *Fourth Sunday in Advent*

At night my soul longs for You, indeed, my spirit within me seeks You diligently; for when the earth experiences Your judgments the inhabitants of the world learn righteousness. *Isaiah 26:9 (NASB)*

Monday, December 21

Blessed are those who hunger and thirst for righteousness, for they will be filled. *Matthew 5:6 (NRSV)*

Tuesday, December 22

A worthless witness mocks at justice, and the mouth of the wicked devours iniquity. *Proverbs 19:28 (NRSV)*

Wednesday, December 23

But the fruit of the Spirit is love, joy, peace, patience, kindness, goodness, faithfulness, gentleness, self-control; against such things there is no law. *Galatians 5:22-23 (NASB)*

Thursday, December 24 - *Christmas Eve*

Thus says the Lord, "In a favorable time I have answered You, and in a day of salvation I have helped You; and I will keep You and give You for a covenant of the people, to restore the land, to make them inherit the desolate heritages." *Isaiah 49:8 (NASB)*

Friday, December 25 - *Christmas Day*

I will put my dwelling place among you. *Leviticus 26:11 (NIV)*

Saturday, December 26

They crush your people Lord; they oppress your inheritance. *Psalm 94:5 (NIV)*

2021

Week 207:
December 27, 2020—January 2, 2021

The greatest necessity of all is to seek out and hold firmly to the truths of our oneness, our hope, our mutual responsibility, our capacity to create, our refusal to destroy. Included here, of course, is a willingness to die, if necessary, for such truths, but not to injure or kill others.

Vincent Harding
Hope and History (99)

Sunday, December 27

Instead of bronze I will bring gold, and instead of iron I will bring silver, and instead of wood, bronze, and instead of stones, iron. And I will make peace your administrators and righteousness your overseers. *Isaiah 60:17 (NASB)*

Monday, December 28

[The wicked] are fat, they are sleek, they also excel in deeds of wickedness; they do not plead the cause, the cause of the orphan, that they may prosper; and they do not defend the rights of the poor. *Jeremiah 5:28a (NASB)*

Tuesday, December 29

For the Lord takes pleasure in . . . people; [God] will beautify the afflicted ones with salvation. *Psalm 149:4 (NASB)*

Wednesday, December 30

For if you truly amend your ways and your deeds, if you truly practice justice between a man and his neighbor, if you do not oppress the alien, the orphan, or the widow, and do not shed innocent blood in this place, nor walk after other gods to your own ruin, then I will let you dwell in this place, in the land that I gave to your fathers forever and ever. *Jeremiah 7:5-7 (NASB)*

Thursday, December 31

I am a stranger on earth; do not hide your commands from me. *Psalm 119:19 (NIV)*

Friday, January 1- *New Year's Day*

May the God of hope fill you with all joy and peace as you trust in [God], so that you may overflow with hope by the power of the Holy Spirit. *Romans 15:13 (NIV)*

Saturday, January 2

When the Lord will have compassion on Jacob and again choose Israel, and settle them in their own land, then strangers will join them and attach themselves to the house of Jacob. *Isaiah 14:1 (NASB)*

Week 208: January 3-9, 2021

The artist who feels called to communicate God's heart for the poor must first learn the joys and struggles of the poor by living among them. As one critic once remarked, "You say you care about the poor? Tell me their names."

Scott A. Bessenecker
Living Mission: The Vision and Voices of New Friars (52)

Sunday, January 3

Like heat by the shadow of a cloud, the song of the ruthless is silenced. *Isaiah 25:5b (NASB)*

Monday, January 4

Why do you plot against the Lord? [God] will make an end; no adversary will rise up twice. *Nahum 1:9 (NRSV)*

Tuesday, January 5

Those who hate me without reason outnumber the hairs of my head; many are my enemies without cause, those who seek to destroy me. I am forced to restore what I did not steal. *Psalm 69:4 (NIV)*

Wednesday, January 6

No one who hopes in you will ever be put to shame, but shame will come on those who are treacherous without cause. *Psalm 25:3 (NIV)*

Thursday, January 7

Redeem me from human oppression, that I may obey your precepts. *Psalm 119:134 (NIV)*

Friday, January 8

Seek good and not evil, that you may live; and thus may the Lord God of hosts be with you, just as you have said! *Amos 5:14 (NASB)*

Saturday, January 9

Like heat in drought, You subdue the uproar of aliens. *Isaiah 25:5a (NASB)*

Week 209: January 10-16, 2021

When we say *shalom*, we utter words the [ruler] does not want to hear.

Walter Brueggemann
Peace (65)

Sunday, January 10

For the whole law is summed up in a single commandment, "You shall love your neighbor as yourself." *Galatians 5:14 (NRSV)*

Monday, January 11

So then, putting away falsehood, let all of us speak the truth to our neighbors, for we are members of one another. *Ephesians 4:25 (NRSV)*

Tuesday, January 12

It is not right to be partial to the guilty, or to subvert the innocent in judgment. *Proverbs 18:5 (NRSV)*

Wednesday, January 13

My soul is weary with sorrow; strengthen me according to your word. *Psalm 119:28 (NIV)*

Thursday, January 14

No, in your heart you devise injustice, and your hands mete out violence on the earth. *Psalm 58:2 (NIV)*

Friday, January 15

I am a foreigner to my own family, a stranger to my own mother's children. *Psalm 69:8 (NIV)*

Saturday, January 16

The alien who is among you shall rise above you higher and higher, but you will go down lower and lower. *Deuteronomy 28:43 (NASB)*

Week 210: January 17-19, 2021

Ultimately a great nation is a compassionate nation. No individual or nation can be great if it does not have a concern for the "least of these."

Martin Luther King, Jr.
Where Do We Go from Here:
Chaos or Community? (178)

Sunday, January 17

Call upon Me in the day of trouble; I shall rescue you, and you will honor Me. *Psalm 50:15 (NASB)*

Monday, January 18

One who secretly slanders a neighbor I will destroy. A haughty look and an arrogant heart I will not tolerate. *Psalm 101:5 (NRSV)*

Tuesday, January 19

So I will deliver you from the hand of the wicked, and I will redeem you from the grasp of the violent. *Jeremiah 15:21 (NASB)*

Bibliography

Ateek, Naim, ed. *The Bible and the Palestine/Israel Conflict*. Jerusalem: Sabeel Ecumenical Liberation Theology Center, 2014.

———. *Justice and Only Justice*. Maryknoll, NY: Orbis Books, 1989.

Barghouti, Omar. *Boycott, Divestment, Sanctions: The Global Struggle for Palestinian Rights*. Chicago: Haymarket Books, 2011.

Bessenecker, Scott A. *Living Mission: The Vision and Voices of New Friars*. Downers Grove: InterVarsity, 2010.

Bessey, Sarah. *Jesus Feminist*. New York: Howard Books, 2013.

Bolz-Weber, Nadia. *Accidental Saints*. New York: Convergent Books, 2015.

Bonhoeffer, Dietrich. *Letters and Papers from Prison*. New York: Macmillan, 1971.

Bonino, José Míguez. *Doing Theology in a Revolutionary Situation*. Philadelphia: Fortress Press, 1975.

Brueggemann, Walter. *Peace*. St. Louis, MO: Chalice Press, 2001.

Carmichael, Amy. *If*. Fort Washington, PA: CLC Publications, 2011.

Chacour, Elias. *We Belong to the Land*. San Francisco: HarperCollins, 1992.

Claiborne, Shane. *The Irresistible Revolution*. Grand Rapids, MI: Zondervan, 2006.

Cleveland, Christena. *Disunity in Christ*. Downers Grove: InterVarsity, 2013.

Cone, James H. *The Cross and the Lynching Tree*. Maryknoll, NY: Orbis Books, 2011.

———. *The Spirituals and the Blues*. Maryknoll, NY: Orbis Books, 1992.

Dawn, Marva J. *Powers, Weakness, and the Tabernacling of God*. Grand Rapids, MI: William B. Eerdmans, 2001.

Day, Dorothy. "The Mystery of the Poor." *Catholic Worker*, April 1964.

———. *On Pilgrimage*, 2nd ed. Grand Rapids, MI: William B. Eerdmans, 1999.

DuBois, W. E. B. *The Souls of Black Folk*. New York: Dover Publications, 1994.

———, and Booker T. Washington. *The Negro in the South*. CreateSpace Independent Publishing Platform, 2015.

Ellis, Carl F., Jr. *Free at Last?* Downers Grove: InterVarsity, 1996.

Emerson, Michael, and Christian Smith. *Divided by Faith*. Oxford: Oxford University Press, 2000.

Evans, Rachel Held. *Searching for Sunday*. Nashville: Thomas Nelson, 2015.

Fasching, Darrell J. *Narrative Theology after Auschwitz*. Minneapolis: Augsburg, 1992.

Foner, Philip S., and Yuval Taylor, eds. *Frederick Douglass: Selected Speeches and Writings*. Chicago: Chicago Review Press, 2000.

Francis. *The Church of Mercy*. Chicago: Loyola Press, 2014.

Grimké, Sarah, and Angelina Grimké. *On Slavery and Abolitionism: Essays and Letters*. London: Penguin Random House, 2015.

Gutiérrez, Gustavo. *Gustavo Gutierrez: Essential Writings*. Edited by James B. Nickoloff. Maryknoll, NY: Orbis Books, 1996.

Harding, Vincent. *Hope and History*. Maryknoll, NY: Orbis Books, 1990.

Harper, Lisa Sharon. *The Very Good Gospel*. Colorado Springs: WaterBrook, 2016.

Hatmaker, Jen. *7*. Nashville: B & H Publishing, 2012.

———. *Interrupted*. Colorado Springs: Navpress, 2014.

Hauerwas, Stanley. *The Peaceable Kingdom*. South Bend: University of Notre Dame Press, 1983.

Ifill, Gwen. "Commencement Address." Wake Forest University, Winston-Salem, NC, 2013.

Irving, Debby. *Waking Up White, and Finding Myself in the Story of Race.* Cambridge, MA: Elephant Room, 2014.

Katongole, Emmanuel. *Mirror to the Church.* Grand Rapids, MI: Zondervan, 2009.

Kelly, Geffrey B., and F. Burton Nelson, eds. *A Testament of Freedom: Essential Writings of Dietrich Bonhoeffer.* San Francisco: Harper & Row, 1990.

King, Martin Luther, Jr. *Where Do We Go from Here: Chaos or Community?* New York: Harper & Row, 1967.

Kraybill, Donald B. *The Upside-Down Kingdom.* 2nd ed. Waterloo, ON: Herald, 1990.

LaCugna, Catherine Mowry. *God for Us: The Trinity and Christian Life.* San Francisco: Harper & Row, 1992.

Legge, Marilyn J. *Liberation Theology.* Maryknoll, NY: Orbis Books, 1992.

Marsh, Charles. *The Beloved Community.* Cambridge, MA: Persius Books, 2005.

McKenna, Megan. *Not Counting Women and Children.* Maryknoll, NY: Orbis Books, 1997.

McLaren, Brian, ed. *The Justice Project.* Grand Rapids, MI: Baker Books, 2009.

Moltmann, Jürgen. *The Crucified God.* New York: Harper & Row, 1974.

Moye, J. Todd. *Ella Baker: Community Organizer of the Civil Rights Movement.* Lanham, MD: Rowman & Littlefield, 2015.

Myers, Bryant L. *Walking with the Poor.* Maryknoll, NY: Orbis Books, 2011.

Newell, Leon. "James Baldwin and Reinhold Niebuhr: Responsibility." *Christianity and Crisis* 47 (1988): 452.

Nouwen, Henri. *¡Gracias!* Maryknoll, NY: Orbis Books, 1996.

———. *The Wounded Healer.* Garden City, NY: Image Books, 1979.

Perkins, John M. *Let Justice Roll Down.* Ventura, CA: Regal Books, 2006.

Placher, William C. *Narratives of a Vulnerable God.* Louisville: Westminster John Knox, 1994.

Rah, Soong-Chan. *The Next Evangelicalism.* Downers Grove: InterVarsity, 2009.

Raheb, Mitri. *Faith in the Face of Empire.* Maryknoll, NY: Orbis Books, 2014.

Romero, Oscar A. *The Violence of Love*. Maryknoll, NY: Orbis Books, 2004.

Said, Edward W. *Culture and Imperialism*. New York: Knopf Doubleday, 1994.

Stevenson, Bryan. *Just Mercy: A Story of Justice and Redemption*. New York: Spiegel and Grau, 2015.

Taylor, Barbara Brown. *Speaking of Sin*. Landham, MD: Cowley Publications, 2000.

Thurman, Howard. *Jesus and the Disinherited*. Richmond, IN: Friends United Press, 1949.

———. *Mysticism and the Experience of Love*. Wallingford, PA: Pendle Hill Pamphlets, 1961.

Tutu, Desmond, and Mpho Tutu. *The Book of Forgiving*. New York: Harper Collins, 2014.

Volf, Miroslav. *Exclusion and Embrace*. Nashville: Abingdon, 1996.

Woodley, Randy S. *Shalom and the Community of Creation*. Grand Rapids: William B. Eerdemans, 2012.

Yoder, John Howard. *The Politics of Jesus*. Grand Rapids, MI: William B. Eerdmans, 1972.

Yousafzai, Malala. "Speech to the United Nations." New York, 2013.

Zaru, Jean. *Occupied with Nonviolence: A Palestinian Woman Speaks*. Minneapolis: Fortress Press, 2008.

CPSIA information can be obtained
at www.ICGtesting.com
Printed in the USA
FSOW02n1128200117
29867FS

9 781594 980381